Succeeding in College
with Attention Deficit Disorders
Issues and Strategies
for Students, Counselors and Educators

Jennifer S. Bramer, Ph.D., L.P.C.

Specialty Pres~ I~~
Plantation, F

Specialty Press, Inc.
300 Northwest 70th Avenue, Suite 102
Plantation, Florida 33317
(954) 792-8100 • (800) 233-9273

Printed in the United States of America

ISBN 1-886941-06-8

Library of Congress Cataloging-in-Publication Data

Bramer, Jennifer S., 1946 –
       Succeeding in college with attention deficit disorders : Issues
and strategies for students, counselors, and educators / by Jennifer
S. Bramer.
       p.   cm.
       Includes bibliographical references (p.   )
       ISBN 1-886941-06-8
       1. Attention-deficit-disordered youth --Education (Higher) --
United States. 2. Learning disabled youth -- Education (Higher) --
United States. 3. College student orientation -- United States.
I. Title.
LC4713.4.B73   1996
371.9 --dc20   96-26196
                                                              CIP

*This book is dedicated
to my daughters, Michelle and Renee,
without whom I would not have had the
inspiration and motivation I needed to persevere.*

ACKNOWLEDGMENTS

I am grateful to many people for their support and assistance with this book. First and foremost, I must acknowledge my husband for his ideas, support, and editorial assistance. I would also like to thank my dissertation committee at Michigan State University, the psychiatrist I call Dr. Samson, the participants in my research study, my friends and colleagues, my publisher and editor, and my family.

I feel so indebted for the work that my husband, Dr. Bob Bramer, has put into this book that I considered including his name as an author. He not only provided me with the encouragement to pursue publication and the emotional support to carry through with it, but he has also edited the manuscript. He has given unselfishly of his time and talents. He is truly a remarkable person and anyone who benefits from this book has him to thank.

I am also indebted to the members of my doctoral dissertation committee at Michigan State University: Dr. Max Raines, Dr. Howard Hickey, Dr. Lou Heikhuis, Dr. Cas Heilman, and Dr. Doug Campbell. This book is based on the research study which was submitted as part of my doctoral degree work. The members of my committee not only provided wise guidance during the time of that study, but also strongly encouraged me to seek publication in book form so that others could benefit from it. I would never have thought of doing that on my own. Their confidence in me, and the value they placed in this subject matter, fostered my ability to persevere.

"Dr. Samson" has been a godsend in my life for a variety of reasons. Without her, the research on which this book is based truly would not exist. She has treated my daughters, educated me about Attention Deficit Disorders, brainstormed with me for specific topics, acted as a subject matter expert, referred her patients to me for participation in the study, and rented me office space to conduct interviews. She is wonderful, and I deeply appreciate everything she has done. (I sincerely regret that I cannot share her real name, but I must maintain her anonymity in the interest of confidentiality for the research participants.)

Additionally, this book would not exist without the time and openness of communication provided by the participants in the study. Because of the constraints of confidentiality, I cannot name them, but I do want to acknowledge them. All of them gave freely of their time, were open and frank in sharing their experiences, and truly wanted to contribute to the research in this field.

I also want to acknowledge the support and contributions of my colleagues and friends in this project. My former Dean, Dr. William Schaar, encouraged me to continue persevering through my doctoral degree, which led to this book. My dear friend, Dr. Joan Hornak, has provided encouragement and inspiration personally and professionally through this project and others for over 25 years. All of my friends have been understanding of my lack of time during this project and have supported me in spirit and with words. I am grateful to all of them. Carolyn Kronenberg provided subject matter expertise for the section on study skills. My colleagues Marianne Robbins and Amy Schaffer have ably assisted with manuscript preparation.

Dr. Harvey C. Parker, my publisher, and Dr. Lynn Wolf, the editor at Specialty Press, have been enormously helpful. Dr. Parker has been enthusiastic and supportive from the beginning of our discussions, has made major contributions to the manuscript, and has facilitated a smooth process. The graphics designer, Sandra Redemske, has added clarity and creativity to my manuscript and book cover. It has truly been a team effort.

Last, but not least, I am gratefully indebted to the other members of my family. The pride of my dad, Richard Schaap, and his undying emphasis on the importance of education have given me motivation forever. My daughters, Renee Irrer and Michelle White, provided impetus for my interest in the subject matter. They along with my stepmother (Charlotte Schaap), my son-in-law (Brent Irrer), and my grandchildren (Tara and Austen Irrer) good-naturedly accepted modifications of holidays and other family times so that I could work. I appreciate their support.

Writing a book is a gratifying, but humbling, experience. It never occurred to me that I might write something such as this during my lifetime. But, then, I had not reflected on the power that several individuals have when they work together on a project sharing their talents, life experiences, encouragement, support, and love. I sincerely want to say "thank you" for our book to all who have contributed.

Jennifer S. Bramer
July 1996

Table of Contents

Contents

Succeeding in College
with Attention Deficit Disorders

Chapter 1

Success is Possible

"Jennifer, what can I say? I shot for the stars and landed on a cloud. My grades came today; I got a 3.0 in Biology, a 3.5 in Algebra, and a 4.0 in my other two classes."

This message on my answering machine a year ago was from Christine—a student I have worked with for several years. I wish every college student hampered by an Attention Deficit Disorder (ADD) could hear her story.

Christine was referred to me for counseling because she was in academic difficulty at the community college where I work and her financial aid was in jeopardy. She desperately wanted to be a pediatric nurse, but was having a terrible time completing and passing the prerequisite classes. I struggled to find appropriate interventions for her through a semester or two, using every resource I could think of at the time—personal counseling, a study skills course, tutoring, etc. Some strategies worked sometimes, but nothing worked consistently. It finally occurred to me that Chris probably had an Attention Deficit Disorder (ADD), undiagnosed and untreated.

After a relatively lengthy process, Chris was diagnosed as having ADD and began treatment, which included counseling, education, and medication. Her academic performance and grades did not improve immediately. She worked with a family therapist on some parenting skills, and then returned to me for counseling on academic and personal issues. In addition, she worked closely with her physician to find appropriate medicine at the correct dosage to treat her attentional problems.

Chris had failed chemistry three times before she finally passed; she had failed biology twice before getting a 3.0 in it. She had to learn to solicit the assistance of the educators with whom she worked. She requested leniency from the college Financial Aid Services and provided documentation that her disability, when undiagnosed, accounted for her unsatisfactory record. She has worked with her college's Office of Disability Support Services to obtain accommodations, tutoring, and books on tape. She talked with her instructors and requested the accommodations she needed to perform successfully in class. Chris has learned to use a calendar for organizing, and to use counseling for coping with emotional barriers and establishing priorities.

This past spring, Chris was selected as one of two students to receive an Outstanding Student Award through the Office of Disability Support Services. She graduated with an associate's degree and has recently been selected, through a competitive admission process, to begin Registered Nurses' training. It has not been a smooth ride to the "cloud" she was on when she left me that message. But she eventually got there and is continuing to pursue her goal.

For students with ADD, a ride on those clouds is seldom quick and easy (and sometimes does not last). I have learned those lessons through my personal and professional experiences (parenting two daughters with ADD who have gone to college, and counseling many college students). But academic success for college students with ADD definitely is possible. Chris is just one success story; there are many others. For an individual with ADD, success like Chris' depends not only on the efforts of the individual with the disorder, but also on the efforts of educators. Students and educators alike must begin their quest for success with an understanding of ADD.

Teachers who understand how ADD impacts their students will be more able, and presumably more willing, to provide appropriate accommodations in the instructional process to assist the student. Counselors who are more aware can provide more appropriate advocacy for the student and can make appropriate referrals for intervention services that may be needed. Students with ADD who understand their disorder can set appropriate expectations for themselves and can more confidently self-advocate, take advantage of available campus services, and utilize coping skills to reach their potential.

Facilitating the development of human potential has been my life work. I have seen, in some of my counselees and in my daughters, how ADD can hamper that development. Bogdan and Biklen (1982) said, "Self-discipline can only take you so far in research. Without a touch of passion you may not have enough to sustain the effort to follow the work to the end, to go beyond the ordinary" (p. 57). My concern for human potential and my ADD-related experiences provided the passion for the research described in this book. My goal in the research was to understand more fully the college experiences of individuals with ADD.

This book was written for both college students with ADD and for counselors and educators who work with them. Background information about ADD, including a discussion of the history, characteristics, causes, and methods of diagnosing the disorder, will provide a basis for understanding this complicated problem. In chapters 5, 6, and 7, stories of seven adults with ADD, who were interviewed as part of an empirical study of college experiences, offer a vivid picture of what it is like to live with ADD. Their personal stories tell us a great deal about the challenges those with ADD face in college, and the success that is within their reach. Information that can empower students with ADD to better help themselves is presented and clinical suggestions for counselors offer practical solutions to assist those with ADD. Methods of treatment, including educational strategies that instructors and administrators can use, are elaborated. I hope the book will help college educators and their students with ADD collaborate in the important work of maximizing the students' human potential.

Chapter 2

ADD—Background and Challenges

"I shouldn't have been accepted into college. I just didn't have the skills to do it."

"There were times when I would wonder if I was smart enough."

"I took the notes; I read; I studied; I did all the things I thought were going to help me, but I was not getting it."

"I couldn't keep up with everybody else."

"I couldn't stay focused. I fell asleep in class."

These statements illustrate the challenges typically faced in college by students who have ADD. While they might question their intelligence, ability, or character as they strive to make their way through school, many of them can succeed and graduate. Christine's dramatic story in Chapter 1 illustrates the claim that success is possible through perseverance and with appropriate treatments and accommodations. An understanding of some general information about ADD and the challenge it presents provides a solid foundation for building student success.

What is an Attention Deficit Disorder?

ADD is a neurological disorder, often thought to be hereditary in origin, which affects the central nervous system. The essential features of the disorder are inattention and/or hyperactivity-impulsivity, more frequent and severe than is typical for individuals at comparable levels of development. (A more complete explanation of the different types of ADD and the history of the terminology appears later in this chapter.) Although ADD is no longer thought of as primarily a childhood disorder, the diagnosis is not given unless some of the symptoms have been present before age seven. Additionally, the features of the disorder must be present in at least two settings—home, school, work. There must also be interference with appropriate social, academic, or occupational functioning.

Inattention

"I really looked attentive, but I'm watching the second hand on the clock behind you or I'm looking at the fly over there or I'm listening to anything ... the clock ticking, the fan running. It could be any number of things."— Mike

One of the primary features of the disorder, inattention, can manifest itself in many ways. People who are inordinately inattentive for their developmental stage probably will find a number of the following things to be true of them. They might:
- have trouble paying close attention to detail
- make careless mistakes; perform messy and careless work
- find it difficult to persist and finish tasks
- appear as if their mind is elsewhere, or they are not lis-

tening, or did not hear what was said
- make frequent shifts from one uncompleted task to another; have difficulty organizing tasks and activities
- find tasks that require sustained mental effort unpleasant
- be easily distracted by extraneous stimuli
- often be forgetful
- initiate frequent shifts in conversation
- not follow the details or rules of games or activities.

Impulsivity-Hyperactivity

"And my mind, my mind was always racing, but I never wanted to look strange so I always had to be in control and appear very relaxed and, so to speak, and don't want to be stared at. I just had to learn that your head is always racing on to the next thing, on to the next, never enjoying the moment. Looking at the clock always; I only have to sit here an hour. If I can sit here for an hour, this will be over, this will pass. I'll be on to the next thing. And feeling that way after only about three or four minutes, it's difficult."— Sally

In addition to having features of inattention, those with ADD might have (but do not necessarily have) features of hyperactivity and/or impulsivity. Russell A. Barkley, Ph.D. (1990), an internationally reknowned expert in the field of attention disorders, advocates that it is really behavioral disinhibition (impulsivity), or a deficiency in inhibiting behavior in response to situation demands, that is the core characteristic for many individuals with ADD. In his work, he emphasizes that problems related to impulsive, disinhibited behavior, more so than inattention, distinguish people with ADD from others.

People who are inordinately hyperactive-impulsive for their developmental stage probably find a number of the following things to be true of their behavior. They might:

- often be fidgety, squirmy in their seats
- have difficulty remaining seated when expected to do so
- have difficulty engaging quietly in activities
- appear to be "on the go" or "driven by a motor"
- talk excessively; feel restless and have difficulty engaging in sedentary activities
- be impatient; have difficulty delaying responses
- blurt out answers before questions have been completed
- have difficulty waiting their turn
- frequently interrupt or intrude upon others
- fail to listen to directions
- initiate conversations at inappropriate times
- touch things that they aren't supposed to, or
- be "accident prone" or engage in potentially dangerous activities.

More males than females are diagnosed with ADD, but people with ADD cover the entire spectrum of intellectual development. Some are gifted intellectually, some are average, and some are slow-learners. Students with undiagnosed ADD often are those who educators sense "are not working up to their potential." Students with ADD often feel frustrated, because they think they should be able to do better but they do not perform well on certain classroom activities.

What Causes ADD?

There are still many unanswered questions as to the cause of ADD. Many experts suspect that a high percentage of those with ADD have inherited it or have developed it as a result of complications during fetal development or birth. Research efforts to attribute ADD to poor parenting, disorganized home environment, lead toxicity, diet, allergies, or emotional factors have not been conclusive.

Most of the evidence for the inheritability of ADD comes from twin, adoption and family studies (Whitman, 1991). Hyperactivity in one twin was found to be correlated highly with hyperactivity in the other, even if they were raised in separate families. Several studies found that concordance of ADD (the disorder existing in both twins) was more frequent in identical twins than in fraternal twins.

Studies comparing adoptive children with their adoptive and biological parents, also, support the inheritability of ADD. If a trait is genetic, adopted children should resemble their biological relatives more closely than they resemble their adoptive relatives. Studies of children with ADD and their parents have found more characteristics of the disorder in their biological parents than in their adoptive parents.

Additional evidence of a genetic basis for ADD is found in studies which examined the rate of occurrence of ADD within a family. It is assumed that the rate of any genetic trait should be relatively high among biological relatives (e.g., brown-eyed people tend to have family members with brown eyes). Investigators who studied families of children with ADD found that ADD tends to run in families much like other genetic traits.

Numerous studies have focused on a possible correlation between ADD and environmental toxins (food additives and dyes, sugar, cigarette smoking and alcohol consumption during maternal pregnancy). As was noted above, the research on diet and ADD indicates that diet does not contribute significantly to the development of symptoms of ADD. It is esti-mated that only a small fraction of people with ADD may have dietary factors as a cause of their symptoms. However, ciga-rette smoking or alcohol intake by the mother during preg-nancy may well lead to neurological dysfunction in a develop-ing fetus resulting in problems such as learning disabilities and ADD.

Investigators have searched for the specific differences in brain function or brain anatomy that may account for ADD. Research has focused on exploring whether disturbances in the production and release of certain neurotransmitter chemi-cals in the regions of the brain which control attention, inhibi-tion, and motor activity may be responsible for causing ADD. A landmark study by Dr. Alan Zametkin and his associates at the National Institute of Mental Health (NIMH) was published in the *New England Journal of Medicine* in 1990. Although it has not been replicated, this study used positron emission tomography (PET) to demonstrate a difference between glu-cose metabolism in a group of adults with ADD and that in a control group of adults without ADD (see photo below).

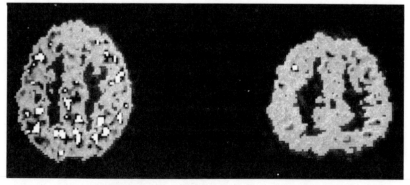

Non-ADHD Adult   ADHD Adult

Note: From "Cerebral glucose metabolism in adults with hyperactivity of childhood onset" by A. J. Zametkin, et al., 1990, New England Journal of Medicine, 323, p. 1365. Copyright© 1990 by The Massachusetts Medical Society. Reprinted by permission.

More recently, using a sample of over 50 boys and girls with ADD, Dr. Judith Rapoport and her colleagues at the National Institute of Mental Health found further evidence that ADD has a neurobiological basis. The investigators used very detailed, precisely analyzed magnetic resonance images (MRI) to compare certain brain structures of a group of children with ADD and those of a control group without ADD. The MRIs showed anatomical differences which, it was concluded, might be indicative of the cause of ADD. Dr. Rapoport explained this finding in a presentation at the Seventh Annual CHADD Conference in November, 1995.

In summary, ADD is widely considered by leading experts to be a neurological disorder which is most likely inherited or the result of problems with fetal development. This explanation is supported by research into the affected areas of the brain in adults and children with ADD. Studies have suggested that differences in neurotransmitter chemicals and in brain structure may be responsible.

Is ADD a New Disorder?

ADD is not a new disorder; however, its name has changed over the years to reflect changes in our understanding of this problem.

The first medical acknowledgment of what is now officially called AD/HD occurred in the *Diagnostic and Statistical Manual of Mental Disorders* (*DSM-II*), published in 1968 by the American Psychiatric Association. The *DSM-II* used the term "hyperkinetic reaction of childhood" to describe children with excessive hyperactivity and stated that this behavior usually diminished in adolescence. There was no mention of its continuation into adulthood.

When the third edition of this manual (*DSM-III*) was published in 1980, the term for the disorder was changed to Attention Deficit Disorder, and three subtypes were identified: ADD with hyperactivity; ADD without hyperactivity; and ADD, Residual Type. The diagnostic criteria reflected three behavioral constellations for defining symptoms: inattention, impulsivity, and overactivity or restlessness. The category of ADD, Residual Type included those individuals (usually adults) who showed signs of attentional deficits and impulsivity which resulted in some impairment of social and occupational functioning and who had (as children) met the criteria for Attention Deficit Disorder with hyperactivity.

In 1987, the American Psychiatric Association published the *Diagnostic and Statistical Manual of Mental Disorders* (*DSM-III-R*), a revised edition of its guidelines for professionals. This time the terminology was changed to ADHD. The 1987 diagnostic manual did not say that the term cannot be applied to adults, nor did it give a specific category such as residual type. This edition included another term, Undifferentiated Attention Deficit Disorder. This was used to describe children who exhibited attentional deficits, but who did not show signs of hyperactivity and/or impulsivity.

The fourth edition of the *Diagnostic and Statistical Manual* (*DSM-IV*), published in 1994, lists three subtypes of the disorder:

- Attention Deficit/Hyperactivity Disorder, Predominantly Inattentive Type
- Attention Deficit/Hyperactivity Disorder, Predominantly Hyperactive-Impulsive Type
- Attention Deficit/Hyperactivity Disorder, Combined Type.

This edition recognizes that when symptoms have been present in childhood, the disorder can persist into adulthood either with a full complement of symptoms, or with less (AD/HD, In Partial Remission). The DSM-IV criteria, listed on page 14, describe the characteristics frequently found in individuals with AD/HD. So, ADD is not a new disorder. However, what is new about ADD is the growing recognition that this problem can affect adults as well as children.

Changes in Terminology Over the Years

1968	DSM-II	Hyperkinetic Reaction of Childhood
1980	DSM-III	Attention Deficit Disorder
		ADD with Hyperactivity
		ADD without Hyperactivity
		ADD, Residual Type
1987	DSM-III-R	Attention Deficit Hyperactivity Disorder
		Undifferentiated Attention Deficit Disorder
1994	DSM-IV	Attention Deficit/Hyperactivity Disorder
		Predominantly Inattentive Type
		Predominantly Hyperactive-Impulsive Type
		Combined Type

In this book, the "generic" term ADD is used to encompass all types of the disorder. Although the disorders manifest in various different ways, there are enough similarities to make some general observations and suggestions.

Diagnostic and Statistical
Manual of Mental Disorders Fourth Edition
Attention-Deficit/Hyperactivity Disorder

A. Either (1) or (2):

    (1) six (or more) of the following symptoms of **inattention** have persisted for at least 6 months to a degree that is maladaptive and inconsistent with developmental level:

    Inattention

    (a) often fails to give close attention to details or makes careless mistakes in schoolwork, work, or other activities

    (b) often has difficulty sustaining attention in tasks or play activities

    (c) often does not seem to listen when spoken to directly

    (d) often does not follow through on instructions and fails to finish schoolwork, chores, or duties in the workplace (not due to oppositional behavior or failure to understand instructions)

    (e) often has difficulty organizing tasks and activities

    (f) often avoids, dislikes, or is reluctant to engage in tasks that require sustained mental effort (such as schoolwork or homework)

    (g) often loses things necessary for tasks or activities (e.g., toys, school assignments, pencils, books, or tools)

    (h) is often easily distracted by extraneous stimuli

    (i) is often forgetful in daily activities

    (2) six (or more) of the following symptoms of **hyperactivity-impulsivity** have persisted for at least 6 months to a degree that is maladaptive and inconsistent with developmental level:

    Hyperactivity

    (a) often fidgets with hands or feet or squirms in seat

    (b) often leaves seat in classroom or in other situations in which remaining seated is expected

    (c) often runs about or climbs excessively in situations in which it is inappropriate (in adolescents or adults, may be limited to subjective feelings of restlessness)

    (d) often has difficulty playing or engaging in leisure activities quietly

    (e) is often "on the go" or often acts as if "driven by a motor"

    (f) often talks excessively

    Impulsivity

    (g) often blurts out answers before questions have been completed

    (h) often has difficulty awaiting turn

    (i) often interrupts or intrudes on others (e.g., butts into conversations or games)

B. Some hyperactive-impulsive or inattentive symptoms that caused impairment were present before age 7 years.

C. Some impairment from the symptoms is present in two or more settings (e.g., at school [or work] and at home).

D. There must be clear evidence of clinically significant impairment in social, academic, or occupational functioning.

E. The symptoms do not occur exclusively during the course of a Pervasive Developmental Disorder, Schizophrenia, or other psychotic disorder and are not better accounted for by another mental disorder (e.g., Mood Disorder, Anxiety Disorder, Dissociative Disorder, or a Personality Disorder). (pp. 83-85)

Code based on type:

    314.01   Attention-Deficit/Hyperactivity Disorder, Combined Type: if both Criteria A1 and A2 are met for the past 6 months.

    314.00   Attention-Deficit/Hyperactivity Disorder, Predominantly Inattentive Type: if Criterion A1 is met but Criterion A2 is not met for the past 6 months.

    314.01   Attention-Deficit/Hyperactivity Disorder, Predominantly Hyperactive-Impulsive Type: if Criterion A2 is met but Criterion A1 is not met for the past 6 months.

ADD is Not Just a Childhood Disorder

Evaluation and treatment of individuals with ADD was long the domain of pediatricians, child and adolescent psychiatrists and psychologists, and pediatric neurologists. Most medical and mental health professionals believed that ADD was a disorder which predominantly affected children, which diminished in adolescence, and which pretty much disappeared by adulthood. Although this pattern did seem to hold true for some people with ADD, there was increasing evidence that not all children with ADD outgrew the disorder.

The likelihood that symptoms of ADD did not always disappear in adulthood came to light in several ways. Upon seeking treatment for their children, parents of youngsters with ADD reported having problems similar to their children's when they were growing up themselves and as adults. Investigators studying family factors in the development of ADD observed traits of ADD in parents when they compared biological and adoptive parents of hyperactive children. Clinicians reported treating adults who experienced a continuation of ADD symptoms from their childhood.

Following hyperactive children into adulthood, Drs. Gabrielle Weiss and Lily Hechtman (1993) found that about 40% to 50% or more of the young adult participants in their study continued to have significant problems with the original symptoms of "the hyperactivity syndrome" and/or social, emotional or personal problems.

Barkley (1990) stated that 50% to 80% of children diagnosed with ADD continue to have some degree of their symptoms in adulthood. Murphy (1992) conservatively estimated that between 2 and 5 million adults may be affected. He said most of these adults with ADD are undiagnosed, untreated, and unaware that help is available. Thus, if we define age 18 as the beginning of adulthood, many more college students than we might have expected are likely to have ADD.

Unfortunately, the knowledge that we do have about ADD in adults is still very weak in research-basis and at this point we can only speculate about all of the effects that ADD has on the lives of adults. There is a growing literature on the subject. In 1991 there were only two books published on the topic of ADD in adults; by 1995, there were fifteen. ADD in adults is often misunderstood and many medical and mental health professionals still do not have knowledge about the existence of ADD in adults, how it affects adult functioning, and appropriate methods used to evaluate, treat and teach adults with ADD. Hopefully, this will change as more research is done and more information becomes available to clinicians and educators. At the same time, the numbers of adults who believe that this disorder has profoundly affected their lives is rapidly expanding and clinical practice in the field is exploding.

How Does ADD Affect Adults?

"I'd sit there, and the prof would be talking or something, and I'd start nodding off. It wasn't because I was tired! I just can't sit through it. I lost interest in it or something."—Calvin

For most people with ADD, symptoms seem to lessen during the years from adolescence to adulthood. Some adults with ADD regard their symptoms as mild and their problems as minor. Others have more serious difficulties and have begun to seek treatment for the disorder since it greatly impacts the quality of their life.

Unfortunately, there have been few studies of adults which shed light on how ADD specifically affects adult adjustment; therefore, we must make inferences from studies with adolescents and from anecdotal reports of adults with ADD. Several investigators (Klein & Manuzza, 1991; G.Weiss & L. Hechtman, 1993; Barkley, Anastopoulas, et al., 1991) reported findings of increased antisocial behavior in adolescents with ADD and continued problems with restlessness and concentration as children transition through adolescence. One study reported that parents and teachers rated adolescents with ADD as being less socially competent, involved in fewer social and organized activities, and having fewer friends (G.Weiss & L. Hechtman, 1993). In self-evaluation the ADD teens rated themselves as better adjusted than their parents and teachers rated them. Yet, they acknowledged significantly more depressive symptoms and antisocial acts than the control group acknowledged. There have been mixed reports with regard to substance abuse, with one study showing a greater likelihood of such abuse among adolescents with ADD and another showing no difference from adolescents without ADD.

Hyperactive children who were followed over a 15-year period into adulthood had less education, more children, more reported sexual problems, more acts of physical aggression, and more suicide attempts than the non-ADD control group. More of the hyperactive group complained of personal problems than the control group. Overall, the most dramatic difference between the adults who had been diagnosed as hyperactive in childhood and the control group was that 66% of the hyperactive group complained of at least one symptom of ADD (restlessness, poor concentration, impulsivity, explosiveness) versus 7% of those in the control group. The researchers concluded that about 50% of the grown-up hyperactive children had fairly good outcome, with some continuing, but not significantly disabling, symptoms. About 50% of them had mildly to severely disabling symptoms (G.Weiss & L. Hechtman, 1993).

There is a great diversity in the backgrounds of adults with ADD, ranging from those who have been highly successful to those who have been extremely unsuccessful in aspects of their schooling, career, social and family life. ADD does not preclude one from becoming successful, but it can create obstacles to reaching one's full potential. Low self-esteem, anxiety, depression and, to a lesser extent, substance abuse are common problems experienced by adults with ADD (Murphy, 1995).

ADD can have an impact on social relationships of adults. Social difficulties may be caused, in part, by impulsivity. Being overly intrusive, forgetful, inattentive, moody and hyperactive can cause a strain on relationships, making it difficult, at times, to keep friends. Others may misinterpret their behavior as rude, self-centered, or irresponsible. Some adults with ADD, having experienced rejection in relationships, withdraw from people to avoid getting hurt again. Many continue to exhibit the same pattern of inappropriate social behavior that has led to this rejection, not realizing how their behavior affects others.

Family life can be seriously impacted by ADD. Ellen Dixon (1995), a clinician who treats many adults with ADD, finds that family life for these people can often be confusing and stressful, the result of problems in such areas as communication, parenting, sharing responsibilities and chores, organizing a household and maintaining routines. For those parents with ADD who have a child (or more than one) with the disorder, the problems multiply.

Problems in the workplace are often reported by adults with ADD. It is not difficult to imagine the variety of problems that can occur at work as a result of impulsivity, distractibility, organizational difficulties, and inattention. Dr. Kathleen Nadeau, the editor of *A Comprehensive Guide to Attention Deficit Disorder in Adults* (1995), provides a list of accommodations that can be instituted in the workplace to help adults with ADD maintain higher levels of efficiency, organization, follow-through, and accuracy in their work.

Many adults with ADD have experienced disappointment in school. Early negative experiences in elementary, secondary school, and college have left them with feelings of inadequacy about their ability to succeed in school. For many, the idea of sitting through lengthy classes, trying to stay alert, and organizing academic projects through to completion is overwhelming and even painful. Thus, many adults with ADD avoid going to school for higher education for fear that they will not be successful.

Not all of the effects of ADD in adulthood, however, are negative. Impulsivity, hyperactivity, and other characteristics of ADD can have a positive side as well. Some adults credit their ADD traits as being responsible for their success. Spontaneity, creativity, limitless energy, flexibility, the ability to handle several different tasks at once, risk-taking, and attraction to novelty and excitement can make adults with ADD quite interesting to be around. As Thom Hartmann (1993) points out, people with ADD may be the "hunters" in our society — risk-takers, entrepreneurs and leaders who often are responsible for the creation of new ideas, social change, and technological and industrial advances. While some places, such as school, may not be the most suitable environment to conduct a "hunt," there are many other places (the marketplace for one) where hunters can thrive and prosper.

The Problem of ADD in College Students

"I didn't want to fail. I <u>did not</u> want to fail. So I found myself reading and rereading. And sometimes I didn't know if I knew what I just read. I wasn't getting a return on my investment. I mean, if I were a stockbroker, I was a failure. I was not getting a good return on my investment."— Mike

When we think about the symptoms listed as features of ADD, it is easy to understand why ADD might cause problems for college students. As a matter of fact, when we think of attributes that contribute to academic success—e.g., close attention to detail, persistence, organization, attentive listening—they are the opposite of ADD characteristics. However, other than the author's recent study which is described in this book, no empirical research has been published about the effects of ADD on college students.

When individuals enter college right out of high school, traditionally they are 18 years old (the legal age for adulthood in many states). Usually they are assuming new adult responsibilities—facing a less structured schedule, having less supervision, caring more for their own personal needs, making more decisions. Also, many college students today are not of traditional age, but are older adults. For these reasons, this book takes the view that <u>all</u> college students are adults.

Barkley (1990) listed 10 complaints of adults who are being evaluated for ADD. Some of those complaints were:
- inability to perform up to intellectual level in school;
- inability to concentrate;
- lack of organization;
- inability to establish and maintain a routine;
- forgetfulness or poor memory;

- confusion, trouble thinking clearly. (p. 614)

Clearly, adults with ADD in college may face formidable difficulties and may need substantial assistance in order to succeed. An observation by Barkley (1990) about the needs of adults with ADD in general is definitely applicable to the needs of college students with ADD. Barkley said:

> Frequently, the significant others in the life of the AD/HD adult must be requested to assist the patient in some of these endeavors, much as parents and teachers of AD/HD children are indispensable to helping the children to be more attentive, more compliant, more reflective, and better organized. (p. 636)

Surely some of the significant others in the lives of college students are educators. Certainly college faculty and staff should be indispensable in helping students through the college experience. To accomplish this, they must acknowledge the effect that ADD may have on student performance in academic settings and provide appropriate services and accommodations to assist them.

ADD is currently being recognized as a disorder which does not disappear with the onset of puberty. College educators and college students must acknowledge the effect that ADD may have on performance in academic settings. In order for students to attain their full potential, educators must be aware of the disorder and provide accommodations to assist students. College students must take responsibility for obtaining an accurate diagnosis, providing documentation to the college, advocating for their legal rights, and utilizing the support services that are available to them. Understanding how the disorder can affect college students is a major part of this process. This book is meant to contribute to that understanding.

Chapter 3

Diagnosis and Treatment of ADD

Although many students who have ADD will have been diagnosed and received treatment prior to entering college, a significant number may be indentified after they have been enrolled. If they have been previously diagnosed, they should consider making that known as early as possible to the campus office in charge of disability services if one exists, or to a college counselor. Students who have not been diagnosed with ADD but who believe they may have symptoms should also consider consulting with the appropriate office. This early contact, for some, could mean the difference between success and failure in college.

Identifying ADD in College Students

ADD in some college students may not have been detected earlier because problems in school may not have been serious enough to require an evaluation. However, as the academic demands increase in postsecondary education, and less structure and supervision are available, symptoms of ADD may become more evident. Furthermore, some students who have had problems with inattention, distractibility, etc. in earlier school settings may have been mislabeled as "lazy," "unmotivated," "sloppy," "spacey," etc. Such labeling often leads students to feel demoralized and discouraged and can result in low self-esteem.

Mary McDonald Richard (1995), of the Office of Student Disability Services at the University of Iowa, noted that many students who experience problems in higher education self-refer or may be referred by college staff or faculty to a university's student disability office. Richard presents common problems leading to such referrals:

- distractibility
- forgetfulness
- boredom
- disorganization
- procrastination
- restlessness
- test anxiety
- low self-esteem
- substance abuse
- relationship problems
- depression
- mood swings
- chronic tardiness or poor attendance
- academic underachievement or failure

When these problems are chronic and persistent, the student may be referred for an evaluation to determine the reason for such difficulties. A proper evaluation may lead to appropriate identification of a student's needs, which could in turn improve the student's chance of success.

Colleges and universities try to be responsive to students with special needs. As more students with disabilities seek higher education, these institutions will become even better equipped and informed to meet diverse student needs. Often, however, it is up to the student to take the first step in seeking assistance. The student must participate in the evaluation process, provide the college any preexisting documentation regarding a disability, and if necessary advocate for legal rights.

How is ADD Diagnosed?

Everyone has times when they are inattentive, impulsive, restless, or disorganized. Individuals with ADD, however, have many of these symptoms much of the time and to a greater degree than would normally be found in the general population.

However, having symptoms of inattention or hyperactivity and impulsivity does not necessarily mean you have ADD, since these same symptoms can be the result of a number of different factors. For example, individuals who suffer from depression, excessive nervousness, or learning disabilities, or those who lack interest or motivation while performing a task, can show problems with inattention, restlessness, or self-control which are not at all due to ADD. A comprehensive evaluation must be done to accurately determine whether a person has ADD.

Diagnosing ADD in adults is not a simple, one-step process. Although there are a number of well standardized measures to assess the presence of ADD symptoms in children and adolescents, there is no such instrument to evaluate adults for ADD. A number of different methods of assessment may be used in the evaluation process. These generally include doing extensive interviews with the individual and collecting data through rating scales and symptom checklists from the client and his/her significant others to accurately define areas of difficulty. Many clinicians also administer psychological tests to measure cognitive processes such as intelligence, memory, attention span, etc. This is especially important for students, since learning disabilities frequently coexist with ADD. Additional medical tests may be ordered to rule out other related conditions that can cause ADD-like symptoms. Below is a list of the kind of information which may be obtained during the assessment process for ADD:

- a developmental history which includes information about the person's early medical, physical, motor, and social development from childhood on;
- a family history checking for other family members who may have problems with hyperactivity, learning problems, substance abuse, or other psychiatric disorders;
- assessment of the person's behavior; the specific symptoms present, their severity and frequency, the degree to which individual symptoms are situational; the duration of the problem;
- psychological and/or educational assessment to determine cognitive ability, whether a specific learning disability is present and, if so, its nature (this is of great importance for remedial educational measures);
- assessment of how the person views himself or herself, family, peers, school; what personality strengths the individual possesses;
- assessment of the interactions between the person and family;
- assessment of the person's academic performance throughout elementary and secondary schools and higher education;
- consideration of the person's neurological status if there is any suspicion of a neurological lesion (routine neurological examinations of hyperactive individuals are usually negative).

As was noted above, some clinicians believe that diagnostic assessment for ADD should always include psychometric (psychological) testing to determine functioning in the areas of mental ability, language, memory, attention span, academic achievement, etc. Others, however, are reluctant to put every adult suspected of having ADD through the rigorous and expensive battery of tests necessary to evaluate cognitive processes like those listed above. In most circumstances, clinicians routinely refer students for such tests if it is suspected that the student may have cognitive deficits which could impair learning and school performance. Such evaluations provide information about the student which could be quite helpful to educators in structuring an educational plan for them in college and identifying areas in need of remediation.

To test for problems of inattention and impulsivity, some clinicians utilize computerized continuous performance tests, for example, the Test of Variables of Attention (TOVA), Conners Continuous Performance Test (CPT), or the Gordon Diagnostic System (GDS). Brown (1995) points out, however, that it is not yet clear how well such "objective" tests can assess the broader range of ADD symptoms.

In reality, professionals have not reached agreement on the best way to conduct an assessment for ADD in adults. Clinicians must do their best to be thorough in their evaluation, ruling out problems of character, mood disorder, alcoholism/substance abuse, anxiety/obsessive compulsive disorder, other neurological problems, medical problems, and learning disabilities.

A rating scale or checklist like the ADHD Behavior Checklist on page 27 by Barkley and Murphy (1995) can be used by

ADHD Behavior Checklist for Adults

Your name _____

Circle the number that best describes your behavior: _____over the past 6 months _____ as a child (5-12 years)

	Never or rarely	Sometimes	Often	Very often
1. Fail to give close attention to details or make careless mistakes in my work.	0	1	2	3
2. Fidget with hands or feet or squirm in my seat.	0	1	2	3
3. Difficulty sustaining my attention in tasks or fun activities.	0	1	2	3
4. Leave my seat in classroom or in other situations in which seating is expected.	0	1	2	3
5. Don't listen when spoken to directly.	0	1	2	3
6. Feel restless.	0	1	2	3
7. Don't follow through on instructions and fail to finish work.	0	1	2	3
8. Have difficulty engaging in leisure activities or doing fun things quietly.	0	1	2	3
9. Having difficulty organizing tasks and activities.	0	1	2	3
10. Feel "on the go" or "driven by a motor."	0	1	2	3
11. Avoid, dislike, or reluctant to engage in work that requires sustained mental effort.	0	1	2	3
12. Talk excessively.	0	1	2	3
13. Lose things necessary for tasks or activities	0	1	2	3
14. Blurt out answers before questions have been completed.	0	1	2	3
15. Easily distracted.	0	1	2	3
16. Having difficulty awaiting turn.	0	1	2	3
17. Forgetful in daily activities.	0	1	2	3
18. Interrupt or intrude on others.	0	1	2	3

trained clinicians in evaluating current and past symptoms of attention deficit disorders in adults. Essentially, the checklist is comprised of the 18 *DSM-IV* items for AD/HD changed somewhat to make them appropriate for adults. Odd numbered items correspond to the "Inattentive Type" symptoms while even numbered items correspond to the "Hyperactive-Impulsive Type" symptoms. Items scored as "Often" or "Very Often" indicate the presence of the symptom. By itself, this checklist should not serve as an indicator of an attention deficit disorder, but it is just one of several assessment tools that can be used by clinicians to make a diagnosis.

How is ADD Treated?

Effective Treatments for ADD: A Multimodal Approach

Optimal success in treating ADD usually is achieved by utilizing several types of treatment simultaneously. Most experts agree that, for best results, a multimodal approach to treatment should be used. Dr. Edward Hallowell (1995) says that treatment for ADD must be comprehensive and may be divided into five components:

1. Diagnosis
2. Education
3. Structure
4. Psychotherapy
5. Medication

He says that diagnosis and education are essential to treatment, that structure is almost always necessary, and that psychotherapy and medication are often necessary.

Diagnosis as Part of Treatment

Treatment obviously must begin with an accurate diagnosis. Many adults self-diagnose when their child is diagnosed or when they are exposed to literature or media on the topic, but a clinical diagnosis by a trained professional is essential. Because of recent media attention to ADD, people often think if they are inattentive or impulsive they have ADD. There are many diagnostic categories which list inattention as a criterion; simply having difficulty concentrating does not indicate ADD. In fact, everyone is inattentive or impulsive at times. An accurate diagnosis of ADD takes into consideration the intensity of the symptoms, their presence since childhood, and whether or not some impairment from the symptoms is present in two or more settings. An accurate professional diagnosis often is therapeutic in itself for an adult with ADD. This diagnosis provides an explanation for years of frustration and underdeveloped potential. With the diagnosis, an appropriate treatment plan can be formed based on the type and severity of ADD, and the ways in which it impacts the individual's life.

Education About the Disorder

Education about ADD for the individual and his/her significant others is essential to all treatment plans. It is important for everyone involved to be exposed to media about the disorder— video and audio tapes, books, pamphlets, articles and speakers. After exposure to the media, individuals and significant others need to reflect (sometimes in the presence of a trained professional) about how this disorder has affected their lives. It is important for adults to reframe the past and their self-images with the knowledge that this is a neurological condition, not a character defect. With that reframing in mind, individuals can begin to work on structuring their lives to accommodate for the impairments created by the disorder.

Structure in One's Living and Learning Environments

A third component of the treatment plan, structure, is almost always necessary. Behavior management strategies must be implemented for the individual to manage the symptoms of the disorder and live more productively. Behavioral strategies are often helpful in dealing with time management, organizational skills, anger control, and communication skills. Individuals must learn self-monitoring and self-rewarding. Many times it is helpful to have a knowledgeable counselor or psychotherapist managing the treatment plan and assisting with the education about ADD as well as the restructuring of one's life. Counselors/psychotherapists can coordinate treatment and monitor behavior management techniques. They can assist the client in making a distinction between those behaviors which are due to the attention deficit and those which are not. They can generate ideas for behavioral management and provide appropriate reinforcement for changes. Often, they can provide career counseling or vocational direction. Although some adults with ADD can structure their own lives after they have been diagnosed and have educated themselves, it usually is helpful to have professional assistance.

Psychotherapy

Psychotherapy, the fourth component of the treatment, is necessary to help deal with coexisting psychological conditions or emotional difficulties and social interactions that are by-products of ADD. For example, anxiety and depression are often present with ADD. Emotional problems such as low self-esteem are often by-products of ADD. Additionally, individuals with ADD often report problems with social situations and relationships.

Many individuals who are diagnosed in adulthood have spent years feeling that they were "different" and that nobody understood them. They have often been criticized for shortcomings resulting from their lack of focus and/or impulsive behaviors. Although many times they know deep down that they have the ability to succeed, they have been unable to actualize these abilities and they know that they are not living up to their potential. They have years of ingrained inappropriate behavior patterns and reinforced negative self-images. Counseling/psychotherapy can empower them to believe that a combination of treatment, support, perseverance and hard work can improve their lives. Experiencing the understanding of a therapist who knows about ADD can be a healing experience. Medication alone is not considered effective treatment for ADD.

Choosing an ADD Specialist
A degree does not tell you much regarding a person's (e.g., physician's, psychologist's, counselor's, social worker's) knowledge about helping people with ADD. You should make sure that you are working with someone licensed or certified in your state. Even a license or certificate, however, does not ensure that a person is prepared to work with individuals with ADD. Experience in dealing with and knowledge about ADD are important. Persons with ADD should make sure to choose professionals who are qualified to help them.

The methods used in counseling clients with ADD can be very different than those used in treating other conditions. It is important for therapists to have knowledge about the proper procedures used to make a diagnosis and to be well-informed about ADD with respect to current legal issues and treatment options. They need to put emphasis on behavioral structuring for the client along with focus on emotional issues. Counselors of individuals with ADD often have to be directive and advice-giving in their approach. They have to assist the client in maintaining focus on specific issues during the counseling session. These methods differ somewhat from traditional psychotherapy and many fine psychotherapists may not realize these differences.

Medications

There has been limited research on how medication affects adults with ADD, However, evidence from research on children and adolescents and clinical reports from practitioners working with adults indicate that pharmacotherapy can be a very effective treatment. Medication is an important intervention to consider in the multimodal treatment planning for adults with ADD. Most children and adolescents diagnosed with ADD take medication to improve attention span, manage hyperactivity or control impulsivity. There have been many studies of the use of medication to treat children and adolelescents with ADD. The results of these studies are usually overwhelmingly positive in confirming the beneficial short-term effects of medication in treating this disorder in children and adolescents. Typically, improvements in attention span, motor activity, impulse control, organization, handwriting, and interpersonal relationships are noted. Academic performance is enhanced. There is good reason to believe that adults with ADD can benefit similarly from medication.

Below is a discussion of medications commonly used to treat ADD. Keep in mind that there has been very little research on the use of these medications with adults. Much of what we know about the effects of medication comes from studies done with children and adolescents.

Stimulants

The most widely prescribed medications for treatment of ADD are the stimulants, which include: methylphenidate (Ritalin®), dextroamphetamine (Dexedrine®), pemoline (Cylert®) and more recently, Adderall® (mixed salts of a single-entity amphetamine product). It is suspected that stimulants have an effect on those parts of the brain which control arousal, regulation of motor activity and impulses. It is generally assumed that stimulants increase alertness by enhancing catecholamine activity in the central nervous system. This is presumed to result from greater availability of specific neurotransmitter chemicals, probably norepinephrine and/or dopamine, at the synapse between neurons. There is some controversy as to the exact site within the brain where these chemical changes take place. Some investigators report portions of the frontal lobe are most involved and others suggest the brain stem is most affected.

The stimulant medications can all be used safely and effectively under a physician's guidance and they can lead to improvements in attention span, concentration, excessive hyperactivity, and self-control. It is estimated that from 50% to 70% of the adults with ADD who take these stimulant medications will find improvement in such areas as ability to focus on school or work assignments, better planning and organization of work, and general increased productivity. The side effects of the stimulants are usually mild and are manageable by adjustments in dosage and timing of administration. Side effects vary and can include problems with sleep, appetite loss, headaches, stomachaches, edginess, and dysphoria. Excessive doses of these medications can produce agitation.

The stimulants, most likely Dexedrine®, Ritalin® and Adderall®, have some abuse potential and are Schedule II controlled drugs, tightly regulated by the Drug Enforcement Administration. At low doses, addiction is not a serious problem. Euphoria is not experienced with oral administration of the stimulants in the dose range typically prescribed. Euphoria, and serious health problems, may occur if these drugs are taken in large doses or are taken intravenously or intranasally.

Antidepressants

Less widely prescribed to treat ADD are the tricyclic antidepressants (TCAs), which include desipramine (Norpramine®), imipramine (Tofranil®) and amitriptyline (Elavil®). The TCAs may have some advantage over the stimulants in the treatment of ADD in that they have a longer half-life, permitting once daily dosing; have low risk of abuse potential or dependence; and may be helpful in adults who do not respond well to the stimulants (Wilens et al., 1995). The use of TCAs has been well researched in children with ADD; however, TCAs have not been extensively studied in a systematic way for treatment of adults with ADD. Side effects of TCAs vary, but the common ones include initial sedation (drowsiness), dry mouth, and constipation. Less common are side effects which are associated with liver function problems and cardiac irregularities. A comprehensive medical evaluation is recommended before starting these medications, and regular monitoring by a physician is necessary.

Selective serotonin reuptake inhibitors (SSRIs), fluoxetine (Prozac®), sertraline (Zoloft®) and paroxetine (Paxil®) have been widely used to treat a number of psychiatric disorders, including anxiety, depression and obsessive-compulsive disorder. Although very beneficial in treating these conditions, they have not been shown to be very helpful in treating the attentional component of ADD.

Antihypertensives

Clonidine (Catapres®) has been found to be helpful in treating children with severe hyperactivity or aggression (Hunt, 1985). It may not significantly improve attention span or distractibility. Clonidine has been primarily used in adults to treat high blood pressure, so its strong hypotensive effects would discourage its use in treating adults with ADD. Guanfacine hydrochloride (Tenex®), another antihypertensive medication, is beginning to see more use in place of clonidine. However, it has not been well studied in either children or adults as a treatment for ADD.

Medication Dosing and Action

All medications are prescribed in a certain dosage to be taken one or more times per day. To have the best effects, the right dosage and timing of the administration of the medicine must be determined. Some medications for ADD work quickly (within 20 to 30 minutes after ingestion) and have a short duration of action, lasting only three to four hours. Others take longer to work and have a longer duration of action which can last all day with continued daily dosing.

Ritalin®, for example, comes in two forms: a standard form and a sustained release form. The standard form, which is usually taken more than once a day, typically starts working within thirty minutes and generally lasts about four hours. A second, third, or fourth dose may be needed during the day to maintain alertness. The sustained release form of Ritalin®, however, may take from thirty to ninety minutes to work, but can be effective for up to eight hours in some people. Therefore, fewer doses may be needed during the day.

Since response to many of the medications described above can vary greatly from person to person, physicians must work closely with anyone taking these medications to adjust dosage and to achieve the optimum effect.

The chart on page 37 provides details about dosing, administration, and effects in children and adolescents of some of the medications discussed.

Medication is Not a Panacea
Medication alone is not considered effective treatment for ADD, but it is often a major component of treatment. Those who are receiving medications should maintain close contact with their prescribing physicians in order to ensure maximum benefits. The physician should monitor main effects and side-effects of the medicine prescribed and adjust the dosage when appropriate. Medication can make things easier for those with ADD, but optimal success often requires multimodal treatment including counseling and education.

Controversial Treatments for ADD
Drs. Barbara Ingersoll and Sam Goldstein (1993) discuss several controversial therapies for ADD. They caution consumers to be wary of treatments which may sound helpful, but which have not been proven to be effective.

Dietary Interventions
Additive-free, sugar-free, and allergen-free diets have all been

Medication Chart to Treat ADD *

DRUG	DOSING	COMMON SIDE EFFECTS	DURATION OF BEHAVIORAL EFFECTS	PROS	PRECAUTIONS
RITALIN® Methylphenidate Tablets 5 mg 10 mg 20 mg	Start with a morning dose of 5 mg/day and increase up to 0.3-0.7 mg/kg of body weight. 2.5-60 mg/day*	Insomnia, decreased appetite, weight loss, headache, irritability, stomachache	3-4 hours	Works quickly (within 30-60 minutes); effective in about 50% of adult patients; good safety record	Not recommended in patients with marked anxiety, motor tics, family history of Tourette syndrome, or history of substance abuse.
RITALIN-SR® Methylphenidate Tablet 20 mg	Start with a morning dose of 20 mg and increase up to 0.3-0.7 mg/kg of body weight. Sometimes 5 or 10 mg standard tablet added in morning for quick start. Up to 60 mg/day*	Insomnia, decreased appetite, weight loss, headache, irritability, stomachache	About 7 hours	Particularly useful for adolescents and adults to avoid needing a noon time dose; good safety record	Slow onset of action (1-2 hours); not recommended in patients with marked anxiety, motor tics, family history of Tourette syndrome, or history of substance abuse.
DEXEDRINE® Dextroamphet-amine Tablet Spansules 5mg 5 mg 10 mg Elixir 15 mg	Start with a morning dose of 5 mg/day and increase up to 0.3-0.7 mg/kg of body weight. Give in divided doses 2-3 times per day. 2.5-40 mg/day*	Insomnia, decreased appetite, weight loss, headache, irritability, stomachache	3-4 hours (tablets) 8-10 hours (spansules)	Works quickly (within 30-60 minutes); may avoid noontime dose in spansule form; good safety record	Not recommended in patients with marked anxiety, motor tics, family history of Tourette syndrome, or history of substance abuse.
CYLERT® Pemoline Tablets (long acting) 18.75 mg 37.5 mg 75 mg 37.5 mg chewable	Start with a dose of 18.75-37.5 mg and increase up to 112.5 mg as needed in a single morning dose. 18.75 -112.5 mg/day*	Insomnia, agitation, headache, stomachache; infrequently, abnormal liver function tests have been reported	12-24 hours	Given only once a day	May take 2-4 weeks for clinical response; regular blood tests needed to check liver function.
TOFRANIL® Imipramine Hydrochloride Tablets 10 mg 25 mg 50 mg	Start with a dose of 25 mg in evening and increase 25 mg every 3-5 days as needed. Given in single or divided doses, morning and evening. 25-150 mg/day*	Dry mouth, decreased appetite, headache, stomachache, dizziness, constipation, mild tachycardia	12-24 hours	Helpful for ADD patients with co-morbid depression or anxiety; lasts througout the day	May take 2-4 weeks for clinical response; to detect pre-existing cardiac defect a baseline ECG may be recommended. Discontinue gradually.
NORPRAMIN® Desipramine Hydrochloride 10 mg 75 mg 25 mg 100 mg 50 mg 150 mg	Start with a dose of 25 mg in evening and increase 25 mg every 3-5 days as needed. Given in single or divided doses, morning and evening. 25-150 mg/day*	Dry mouth, decreased appetite, headache, stomachache, dizziness, constipation, mild tachycardia	12-24 hours	Helpful for ADD patients with co-morbid depression or anxiety; lasts througout the day	May take 2-4 weeks for clinical response; to detect pre-existing cardiac defect a baseline ECG may be recommended. Discontinue gradually.
CATAPRES® Clonidine Tablets Patches .1 mg TTS-1 .2 mg TTS-2 .3 mg TTS-3	Start with dose of .025-.05 mg/day in evening and increase by similar dose every 3-7 days as needed. Given in divided doses 3-4 times per day. 0.15-3mg/day*	Sleepiness, hypotension, headache, dizziness, stomachache, nausea, dry mouth, localized skin reactions with patch.	3-6 hours (oral form) 5 days (skin patch)	Helpful for ADHD patients with co-morbid tic disorder or severe hyperactivity and/or aggession.	Sudden discontinuation could result in rebound hypertension; to avoid daytime tiredness starting dose given at bedtime and increased slowly.

* Dose varies from individual to individual. Medications should only be prescribed by a physician. Information presented here is not intended to replace the advice of a physician. <u>Note</u>: From "Medication Chart to Treat Attention Deficit Disorders" , 1993, by H. C. Parker. Copyright © 1993 by Specialty Press, Inc.

proposed to solve problems of hyperactivity and inattention in children. Dr. Benjamin Feingold's (1975) book, *Why Your Child is Hyperactive*, popular in the late 1970's, caused many doctors to prescribe special elimination diets for hyperactive children. Dr. Feingold claimed that naturally found salicylates in foods and artificial food flavorings and colorings caused symptoms of hyperactivity, learning problems and attentional difficulties. With testimonials by many parents who believed they saw differences in their children with the diet, Dr. Feingold's theories became very popular. They were not, however, able to withstand the scrutiny of many well controlled studies which failed to find the elimination diet to be an effective treatment for ADD. There is also a lack of controlled studies proving a relationship between allergies and ADD, and there is no evidence to indicate that sugar in the diet of children exacerbates hyperactivity or attentional difficulties.

Orthomolecular Therapy

Orthomolecular psychiatry advocates the use of vitamins and minerals in the treatment of certain mental disorders. This treatment is based on the theory that, for some people, a genetic abnormality results in an unusually high need for certain vitamins and minerals, a deficiency of which can result in mental illness. Proponents of orthomolecular treatments claim that hyperactivity and learning disabilities in a child can be successfully treated by supplementing the child's diet with specific vitamins and minerals. While it is true that vitamin deficiencies can result in certain health problems and serious diseases such as scurvy, pellagra, and rickets, there is no evidence that ADD or learning disabilities are caused by such deficiencies. Both the American Psychiatric Association and the American Academy of Pediatrics have concluded that megavitamin therapy is of no benefit in the treatment of either of these dis-orders.

Anti-Motion Sickness Medication

Proponents of this treatment claim that ADD is caused by dis-turbances within the inner ear which affect the vestibular sys-tem and that certain medications can be used to correct this disturbance, thereby correcting the ADD. There is no scien-tific evidence to link problems with attention or impulsivity-hyperactivity to the inner ear system. However, advocates of this treatment have written extensively, providing anecdotal claims that patients with ADD and learning disabilities have been treated effectively with anti-motion sickness medications. No controlled study has proved this treatment to be effective for these populations.

Candida Yeast Treatments

Some have claimed that the overgrowth of candida albicans in the body can weaken the immune system, increasing suscepti-bility to many illnesses, including ADD. Their treatment is the administration of antifungal medications and a reduction of sugar in the diet to slow yeast growth. While candida can cause infections of the vagina, mouth, and skin, proponents of this theory offer no scientific research to back their claims regard-ing ADD. Instead they provide only questionable anecdotal reports of successful management of ADD with this treatment.

EEG Biofeedback

EEG biofeedback is a technique for measuring levels of elec-trical activity in the brain and feeding this information back to the patient via unique signals which the patient is trained to manage and control. The theory behind EEG biofeedback is consistent with theories about low levels of arousal in the brain found in people with ADD. When trained with EEG biofeedback, children with ADD learn to increase certain desirable brain wave activity. There have been an insufficient number of controlled studies providing evidence that EEG biofeedback training leads to improvements in attention, hyperactivity or impulsivity in children with ADD. The treatment can be very time-consuming and costly, as training may require from 40 to 80 treatment sessions over a three- to six-month period and may not yield any lasting results.

Neural Organization
This is a technique used by chiropractors to correct misalignments in the body that they claim can produce learning disabilities and ADD. These misalignments, they say, can be the cause of neurological dysfunction due to unequal pressure being exerted on different areas of the brain. Treatment consists of manipulation of the body in specific ways so as to restore the cranial bones to their correct position. There is no research to support the conclusion that neural organization is effective in the treatment of ADD.

Optometric Vision Training
Optometric training is espoused by a group of developmental optometrists as a treatment for learning disabilities caused by faulty eye movements and failure of the eyes to focus together properly. Treatment usually consists of eye exercises and perceptual training designed to correct these problems. Although it would seem logical to assume that visual disorders may be an underlying cause of learning difficulties (especially reading problems), researchers have found learning disabilities to

be the result of language processing deficits rather than problems with the visual system. Visual training has not been found to be an effective treatment for ADD.

(The sections on "Medications" and "Controversial Treatments for ADD" were contributed by Dr. Harvey C. Parker, who drew not only from his own knowledge, experience, and previously published work, but also from the work of others: the authors cited, E.D. Copeland and S.C. Copps [1995] and L.B. Silver [1992].)

Summary

Awareness of ADD has grown enormously over the past ten years, and with that growth a variety of treatments have been proposed to benefit those with this condition. With such a wide variety of choices to make, people with ADD need to be educated consumers. They need to be aware of those treatments which have proven to be effective and those which have not. Fortunately, scientists have been very busy over the past twenty-five years doing ADD research, so we know pretty well what works and what doesn't with children and adolescents. Most clinicians believe that most adults with ADD derive benefit from treatment programs which include counseling, medication, accommodations in the school environment or workplace, and education about ADD. Treatments which are unproven or controversial may end up being a drain on resources, both time and money.

Chapter 4

Interviews
About College Experiences

As a mother of two young adults with ADD who were in college and as a college counselor who had observed ADD symptoms in many students, I became interested in knowing how college was experienced by those with ADD. To find out, I conducted extensive interviews with seven adults who had been diagnosed with ADD and collected data about their college experiences and the ways in which they dealt with them. For those readers who are interested, the questions asked and methodology used during these interviews can be found in Appendix E.

As their stories in chapters 4, 5, and 6 will show, college was not easy for any of the students interviewed for this study, but success has by no means been beyond their reach. With only one exception, they have become convinced that diagnosis for ADD and appropriate treatment could have made, or did make, a very great difference in their pursuit of success in college.

For many students with ADD, school is not easy to cope with; college can be worse. Often students move away from supportive home environments when they go away to college. At the same time the educational environment is less structured. The challenges presented in college can batter self-esteem, which often is already fragile. Sometimes students flounder, performance declines, and self-esteem plummets.

Some of the individuals I interviewed had the benefit of diagnosis and treatment for their ADD while they were in college, and others did not. Whether it occurred while in college or later, all but one of them valued treatment, including medication, in their efforts to achieve success and fulfillment. And whether diagnosed and treated in college or not, several of them identified experiences which were notably helpful in college. One experience was working with faculty whose style provided acceptance and support. Another positive experience was utilizing support services such as tutoring and counseling. Still other helpful experiences were visual and "hands-on" learning activities, and using study environments which helped the individual students maximize concentration. The insights of these individuals can be encouraging for others in college who have ADD.

Seven participants provided information for this study. All seven were Caucasian. Two were female; five were male. They all had entered college immediately after high school, and some also attended college later on. They all had been diagnosed with ADD by the same psychiatrist. None of them had any other major psychiatric diagnosis; however, two participants said they had been diagnosed with learning disabilities (and one was unsure). See page 44 for a summary of the participants' demographic characteristics.

The adults in the study were diagnosed several years ago, according to the third edition of the *Diagnostic and Statistical Manual of Mental Disorders* (*DSM-III*) of the American Psychiatric Association (1980). They met the diagnostic criteria for Attention Deficit Disorder, Residual Type, code 314.80. The psychiatrist who diagnosed them used a 2-hour in-depth clinical interview. During this interview she sought to gather

Demographic Characteristics of the Study Participants

Name	Current Occupation	Initial Educational Goal	Educational Attainment Before Drop-out	Highest Educational Attainment	When Diagnosed and Treated for ADD	Reported a Learning Disability	Attend College After Treatment
Calvin	Electronics technician	Undecided-later, paramedic degree	Welding classes at community college	EMT training; some paramedic training	June 1993; 3-4 months before interview	No-never tested	No
Keith	Owner of multiple businesses	Bachelor's degree-undecided major	1 year small state university	1 year university	6-9 months before interview	No-never tested	No
Sally	Homemaker	Bachelor's degree-teaching	2 years small private college	2 years small private college; 1 year vocational school	March 1993; 7-8 months before interview	Yes-dyslexia	No
Tim	Prison guard, desktop publishing business	University degree-photography	1 term community college; 1 term state university-AA degree law enforcement	Bachelor's in nontraditional program for returning adults	About 2 years before interview	No-never tested	Uncertain
Mike	Sales representative for manufacturing plant	Law degree	Bachelor's degree, small private college; 1 year law school	1 year law school	About 10 years before interview	No-never tested	Specific interest classes
Dale	Computer technician for major university	Bachelor's degree-music?	3 years community college, bachelor's degree in telecommunications	Bachelor's degree in telecommunications major university	During community college-about 6 years before interview	Not sure	Yes
Kathy	Medical student	Bachelor's degree from private university	1 semester private university, enrolled in another private college	Bachelor's degree, small state univeristy; 3rd year medical school major university	During 1st year in medical school-almost 2 years before interview	Yes	Yes

the following type of information:

- their medical history and the medical history of other family members;
- symptoms of other conditions which might present like ADD, such as anxiety, depression, substance abuse, endocrine abnormalities, menopause, thyroid or estrogen imbalance;
- their educational history, employment history, and assessment of current functioning;
- symptoms they related to when they read either *The Hyperactive Child, Adolescent, and Adult* by Paul Wender, M.D. (1987) or *Attention Deficit Disorder in Adults* by Lynn Weiss, Ph.D. (1992).

Most of the individuals in this study (at least four) had not yet been diagnosed and treated for ADD when they were in college. Two were diagnosed and treated during their college careers. One was not certain when he was diagnosed, but thought it was during his last year of college, perhaps shortly before he completed it. Their amounts of college experience covered a wide spectrum. Two had a year or less, and one had two years. Two had bachelor's degrees, and one had a bachelor's degree plus a term of law school. One was in her third year of medical school at the time of the interviews. In order to assure anonymity and confidentiality, information which might identify the participants has been changed. For example, pseudonyms have been used for their colleges and for the organizations where they have worked. However, their experiences have not been altered substantively.

In some ways the opinions these seven individuals related to me were vastly different. In other ways they were similar. Some common threads emerged when I talked with them. Some of the feelings and experiences they expressed will ring true for others with ADD who have gone to college. Hopefully, their stories will provide hope and inspiration to those who are struggling.

Chapter 5

A Year or Two of College Produced Various Results

Calvin

"My fortune is the fact that I have found something to make a profession out of, something I love to do."

From High School Expulsion to Electronic Technician

Calvin was a 38-year-old electronics technician at a national industrial corporation at the time of my interviews with him. He had not completed high school, but had attended some welding classes at the community college. He had successfully completed emergency medical technician training at the same college, but then dropped out of the paramedical training that followed. He never had been tested for learning disabilities and was not aware whether he had any. He had been diagnosed with ADD three or four months before my first interview with him and had not attended any college classes after treatment.

Calvin told me he had low self-esteem as a child. He said he had needed to repeat the second grade. I said, "Do you remember how you felt about yourself? Like, when people were making reference to you having been held back, to being stupid, to being lazy, those types of things. Do you remember if you believed them or not?"

"Yeah. I believed them. I mean, at that age. I had very low self-esteem. I was overweight, too, and that didn't help any."

Calvin had experienced problems all the way through school, and didn't complete high school with his class.

At that time his goal was unclear. He was expelled from high school for behavior problems. About two years after he was expelled, he took some welding classes at the community college. Later, he completed emergency medical technician (EMT) training. After the EMT training, he began an associate's degree in paramedic training, but never finished it.

Calvin told me the story like this: "I went for a semester of welding type of stuff. My dad owned a machine shop, and he got a chance to teach down there at CCC, so I took a class with him and ended up teaching some of the class myself. I knew more than those people.... I went into emergency medical technician training in '78, I think. And then in 1980 I went into paramedic training. And at that point I was going through a divorce so I never finished. I got through one term, and that was about it."

Calvin's experiences in college were probably colored by his expertise in the subject matter. Not only did he have related work experience before he took the welding class, he also had work experience in emergency medicine before he pursued classes in it. A little later in his life, after he had been working as a police officer and doing volunteer emergency medical work for a while, he completed emergency medical technician training at the community college.

*****

Since Calvin told me that his self-esteem had been low when he was a youngster, I asked about his self-esteem during his emergency medical technician (EMT) training. He replied,

"Well, I would say it was pretty good, actually. I was extremely confident in what I was doing. I had a lot of support from co-workers and people that I worked with. They would let me do things that they wouldn't let other people do. They were confident in my abilities and I was, too. So, as far as that goes, I felt pretty good about that."

We didn't talk specifically about his self-esteem during other periods of his college career. However, Calvin had dropped out of paramedic training and never went back.

Calvin had struggled academically: he had been "kicked out" of high school, and didn't extend his education (other than one welding class) until he entered college when he was older. He told me about the pressure he felt in classrooms, pressure which could be either exacerbated or alleviated by the personality of the instructor. He said, "I felt pressured because I might get called on and not know the answer. I feel pressured because I don't know these students and I don't know this instructor. I'm uncomfortable and I'm thinking of all these things that could go wrong."

Calvin talked about an emergency medical technician instructor whom he had known ahead of time.

During this discussion, I said to Calvin, "Several people have told me that the personality or attitude of instructors they had in class made a big difference. It sounds like in this case it made a difference because you didn't feel the pressure or intimidation; you didn't have to prove yourself."

"Right, right," Calvin responded.

"Do you remember any other classes where the instructor made a difference?" I asked.

He told about his cardiology instructor: "She was one that, if you didn't know it, she'd just pick at you, chip at you. . . . It just made that, 'Oh, my God!' you know, a hundred different things go zipping through my head." He said he had a lot of problems with her.

The other instructor's personality, Calvin said, created a much more positive atmosphere for him to learn in. He said, "That was much more laid back because that was her personality. She was an R.N. and the whole nine yards, and she was a very easy person to get along with. She wasn't so inclined to make you feel little because you didn't know it right then and there."

"And the other one, the one that picked at you?" I asked. "One of the feelings that you had, at least with her, was feeling belittled?"

"Yes, very much so, because then I'd feel inadequate and the whole nine yards." Calvin responded.

When I asked him to describe that experience, he said, "Like, ah, what the other people in the class were thinking, will I ever get through this? A lot of stressful feelings that I can remember. My hands would start sweating and I'd almost start shaking."

*****

The first time I interviewed Calvin and asked about his preferred study environment, he said, "I really had no study environment. I mean, I didn't have any set way to study. Truthfully, I don't remember studying that much."

During my second interview with him, I pushed him a little harder to describe his ideal study environment. I said, "If you had to study, do you remember where and what was most comfortable for you? Like some people say that they want absolute quiet; some people say they can't stand it to be real quiet; they have to have some background noise. Some people say they want to be isolated, but with people around. Can you relate to any of that?"

To this, Calvin responded, "... I needed to be alone by myself, quiet, no distractions, nothing, no TV, no nothing. Normally I'd go into the bedroom; I'd sit on the bed and try to read. I could never ... and I tried to sit at the kitchen table and try to work; that never worked."

"Why?" I asked.

"Distractions," Calvin responded.

"Other people around?"

"Other people," Calvin confirmed. "I'd hear something, and then I'd start thinking of something, and then I was lost on what I was doing."

Calvin also told me his mind wandered in class; he said he just got bored.

Calvin is definitely a visual learner, with a preference for hands-on experiences. When I asked him what types of classes he preferred in college, he said, "The hands-on stuff, actually doing injections, actually drawing the fluids, things of that nature; the hands-on was much better than sitting through two hours of lecture on the pharmacology and that type of stuff. Cardiology was interesting because we got to do hands-on stuff running strips, run EKGs; that was pretty interesting. Anything that was hands-on."

Calvin also told me about hands-on learning that he does even now in his career as an electronic technician. He said he rarely reads instructions when he assembles something, and when he designs something he often builds it before drawing it on paper.

*****

Calvin has found success and satisfaction in a field different from the course of study he began in college. At the time of my interview with him, Calvin had been working in the electronics field for about twelve years and had been employed by Sesmo Industrial for nine years. This is the way he explained his occupation: "I work with a lot of high-tech electronics computer-based equipment. Electronics has always been my hobby, and I got into the profession in 1981 doing it full-time and I've just stayed in it ever since. I went to work out here at Sesmo; I'll be starting my ninth year. I'm a senior technician, and I do a lot of troubleshooting with what other people can't figure out. I work a lot with computers. I do a lot. I maintain a lot of the equipment; plus I'm the technical director. I set up everything. I make sure all the computers are right."

It seems Calvin has mastered a very complex job far removed from all his early occupational goals: welding, emergency medical technician, and paramedic.

Not only has Calvin found success in what he does, he also has found satisfaction. When we were talking about his current job, he said, ". . . I don't get bored with it. . . . I can sit down at computers and you can bring me in any equipment, I can repair it whatever...."

Reflecting, I told Calvin it seems that many people with ADD find something they really like to do and are successful and focused within their fields.

Calvin agreed with my analysis. He said, "I can sit—if I didn't have any other distractions or anything else—I could sit from the time I get up in the morning until the time I drop at night with my computer work or my electronics work, period.

That's it. Now, you ask me to do something else and you might as well forget it 'cause I'm going to sit around and procrastinate 'til hell freezes over. Not because I can't do it, because I just get into it and I'm into it and I cannot stay focused on it."

A few minutes later, Calvin made it perfectly clear that he is not only successful but also satisfied. He said, "My fortune is the fact that I have found something to make a profession out of, something I love to do."

*****

Calvin had been away from college about fifteen years when his ADD was diagnosed. Reflecting on the loss he feels about not being diagnosed earlier, he said, "I mean, I look back and if I would have been on Ritalin or any medication at that time when I was coming up through school, I know I would not have had any problems in school. I would probably have been able to go to college and get a degree in something...."

I summarized what I thought I had heard him expressing. I said, "I sense that what you're thinking now is that you wouldn't have any problem. I mean, if you could drop everything, if time and money were no object and you could go to school now, you could do whatever you want to do. Is that what you're feeling?"

"Yeah," Calvin replied." I feel I could accomplish at least a four-year, easy."

"Whereas before?" I asked.

"No way! Overwhelming," Calvin responded.

Keith

"If you go into treatment and you start treating yourself for this, then all of a sudden all of these doors open. All of these doors open for interests that, geez, 'I can do this now, I can do that now, I can do that now.' You can do all of these other things."

Hyperactivity: an Asset in Business

Keith was a 35-year-old owner of multiple businesses. He was not aware of ever having been tested for learning disabilities. He had been diagnosed and had begun treatment for ADD six to nine months before my interviews with him. He had not attended any college classes after his diagnosis.

Keith had a clearly established goal when he graduated from high school, and he did attend Southfield State University for one year, presumably to pursue a bachelor's degree. He went that one year and then left to accept employment. He never returned.

*****

Among those I interviewed, Keith was one possible exception to the observation that college experiences often diminished self-esteem. I asked Keith, who is relatively well-read about ADD, "Do you see yourself as having more or less friends than the 'average Joe'?"

"Many more," was his quick response. "And I know everybody. I know everybody."

"Okay," I responded understandingly.

"Okay? That's what everybody says about me. No matter where I go, I run into somebody that I know."

"Um, I sense you feel real comfortable with yourself, and that you're not having any self-esteem problems," I observed.

Keith laughed and replied rhetorically, "How could you tell?"

I laughed and continued, "We often talk about the self-esteem problems that ADD people have."

"They have extremely low self-esteem," Keith said.

"You see yourself as an exception to that?" I asked.

"Yes, I do," Keith said. He explained: "I am very different. Because of my father. My father had this attitude, 'You get knocked down; you get back up; you try something else. There's a ton of room in this world for you, Keith; you just find it.' I mean, when somebody tells you that, that's pretty great."

Keith was satisfied with his academic success in college. Although he attended only one year, he did not drop out because of academic standing or struggle. In fact, he earned better grades at the university than he had in high school. He attributed his success to luck in getting certain professors.

He said, "Considering what my high school was like, you know, I think I did quite well. I was really happy with it. I got lucky. Really lucky. I had some great professors up there. I had a professor that taught me how to read."

Keith described two of his university teachers who made a keen impression on him. First he described a speed-reading teacher: "This old bird took me under his wing and he taught me how to read. I remember him and the physics teacher I had. And he taught me how to read and he taught me how to speed read. He taught me how to sort and pick and do everything that you needed to do to read. From then on, man, I was just a reading idiot."

Keith elaborated: the instructor had taught him "to get the main topics and cull the information and just pass over the stuff that's trivial." He said that what the instructor had changed was his attitude about reading. He said that previously he had hated to read, but "now I can't find enough to read. I read while I'm standing mixing feed. I read while I'm going down the road." Summing up his memories of his reading teacher, Keith said, "It was only six weeks, but it was the best six weeks I had."

Keith also told about his physics teacher, whose personality and attitude made a strong impression on him. When Keith registered for the class it had a rather vague course title, and he didn't realize it was a physics class until after the drop and add period was over. When he realized that he had registered for a physics class, he reacted aloud in class and the instructor told him to stay after class. Keith told me the story:

"So I stayed and he said, 'What's the problem?'

I said, 'My God, I've never had physics before in my life; I just struggled my way through biology. What am I going to do? I can't get out of your class now. I paid all of this money. What am I going to do? This is physics, oh my gosh, oh my God.'

He said, 'Do you live on campus?'

I said, 'Yes.'

He said, 'Well, I'm in this lab every night until 10:00. What I'd like you to do is, tomorrow, come on down. If you've got your readings, you've got your information. If you don't understand anything, come on down.'"

Keith went on, "Well, it took about three weeks and I was setting up all the lab experiments for him, was doing everything in front of the class with him. What he did, he would teach it to me while we were setting up the project."

Summing it up Keith said, "It's exactly the same old thing of somebody not knowing exactly what they are doing for a student, but he took me under his wing and he said, 'These are the concepts.'"

Keith said that both the reading teacher and the physics instructor made a difference in his life because they displayed a caring attitude and were able to extract the most important concepts for him.

In a later interview, Keith talked about the type of lecturer he thought made an impact: "What it takes is for someone to get up in front of class and have a little bit of stimuli to them. Then we're 'suck city'; anything that comes out of their mouth gets pulled right in." Referring to the physics instructor, he said, "He had tons of fire. That man was a walking firecracker waiting for him to explode all the time. I learned a lot. He was good. We never had an empty seat in that class. Everybody came to that class."

*****

Keith did not complain of a lack of focus while studying as much as some of the other interviewees did, but he did mention it. He said he had more difficulty studying in the dorm than he did when he was out on the road playing with his band. He said, "I did better on the road than in the dorm. In the dorm I'd get screwing around."

When Keith described his ideal study environment, he described the circumstances in his life at the time of our interview. Even though he was not then in school, he did a significant amount of reading and public speaking. Keith does not take medication constantly, but only when his daily activities seem to demand it. He described needing a different kind of study environment when he was off medication than when he was on medication. He said, "But if I really want to sit down and I want to get a presentation ready, I want to research a lot of information, and I want this something to be put together real well, I'll take my Ritalin; I'll sit down and read my information...."

I asked him, "So, no noise is better for you than noise?"

He said, "Yeah, well for me, when I'm on Ritalin. When I'm not, it doesn't matter. But, well, because, see you're not completely focusing when you're not on Ritalin, right? So outside noise is just stimuli for you."

I asked him how it was when he was in college (which was before he was diagnosed and treated): "You didn't try to have a quiet environment to learn things?"

"No," he said, "I couldn't take it... I couldn't take a quiet environment."

Keith also stated a preference for visual and hands-on learning. He attributed the preference to his poor reading skills. He said, "If you're a poor reader, you have to have some way to take the material in." He also referred again to the positive experience with his physics teacher, who had Keith assist with the laboratory demonstrations. Keith learned that way. Other subjects he enjoyed were photography and graphic arts, project-oriented classes.

Keith mentioned doodling and sleeping, also. When we were discussing his preferences in instruction, he began talking about boring lecturers. I asked, "What happens when you get in a class like that?"

He replied, "Zzzzzz," feigning a snoring sound and closing his eyes, " . . . or draw or play doodle."

Keith didn't think the university he attended offered any support services so he never sought any.

*****

At the time of our interviews, Keith was the owner/operator of multiple businesses. He owned a fifty-acre farm, a motel, and a manufacturing company. Although he was currently a little bored, by his own analysis, he was successful in what he was doing. Referring to his manufacturing business, he said, "I've been in it for four years now. I went from nothing to producing fifteen thousand a week; so, which is for one guy …."

"Fifteen thousand?" I interrupted for clarification.

Keith confirmed it: "Fifteen thousand, a week, yeah. It's good; it's good money. I mean, I have a forty percent profit margin; I make forty percent. Other companies usually make nine percent, ten percent, fifteen percent…."

Then Keith reflected that he is getting a little bored with what he is doing. He said, "I love stimulation, it's not exciting any more. This is a great business; I have a tremendous income from it. My motel does well, too. That's another one of my businesses, a motel. And that does real well. I'm just kind of in a rut, kind of bored."

Laughing, I said, "Time to start a new business, Keith."

"Yeah," he said, "there ain't nothing I can't do."

Discussing his success in life, he said he thought he compared favorably to his siblings.

With pride in his voice, he told me, "I had two sisters and two brothers. Two of them had masters', one a Ph.D., and one a bachelor's—all from Big Ten universities. I am the black sheep, okay? …When it comes to 'You'll never get this and you're not smart enough, you know you can't do that, and geez, you're not going to be successful and on and on.' Well, my income is twice what theirs is."

Although Keith wasn't completely satisfied with his current occupations, he considered himself successful.

*****

Keith had been away from college for approximately fifteen years when his ADD was diagnosed and his treatment began. He was not speaking about college specifically when he described the benefits of diagnosis and treatment, but I believe his comments are applicable. He said, "If you go into treatment and you start treating yourself for this, then all of a sudden all of these doors open. All of these doors open for interests that, geez, 'I can do this now, I can do that now, I can do that now.' You can do all of these other things."

A few minutes later, Keith said, "See, I would love to go back to college."

"Would you?" I responded.

"Hell, yes," he said." Oh, yeah. First thing I'd like to try, I'd like to try a broadcasting course."

A few minutes later he said, "I'd love to do what Dr. Samson does. I'd love to be a psychologist or a child psychologist, you know. I don't think I'd want to be a psychiatrist, I don't have enough years left in my life to complete the studies. Thirty-five years old, man."

When I reflected that he had a long time ahead of him and lots of energy, he said, "That's right. I've got all kinds of time to be successful in a number of different things."

Keith felt that "doors opened" for him after he got treatment, and that he could be successful if he went back to college.

Sally

"I just had to learn that your head is always racing on to the next thing, on to the next, never enjoying the moment. Looking at the clock always; I only have to sit here an hour. If I can sit here for an hour, this will be over, this will pass. I'll be on to the next thing. And feeling that way after only about three or four minutes, it's difficult."

Beautiful and Bright, but No Confidence

Sally, an extremely attractive 34-year-old homemaker, had long dark hair and was fashionably groomed at the time of our interviews. When she first graduated from high school, she wanted to earn a bachelor's degree and become a teacher. She attended a small private college for two years and dropped out; several years later she attended one year at a vocational school. She said she was dyslexic in math. She had been diagnosed with ADD and had begun treatment about seven or eight months before our interviews. She had not attended any college classes since her diagnosis.

Much of Sally's academic life was a struggle. She told me an amazing story. She remembered trying to isolate herself in the first grade so that she could concentrate in her classroom. She told me, "Even in the first grade, I remember putting up all my books around the desk to block myself in by myself to concentrate. But they wouldn't allow me to do that. But I remember doing that now, and I think back that it was because I was trying to keep everybody out so I could zero in on my papers. I just could not concentrate."

At least at an early age, she thought isolation would create a helpful study environment.

Sally told me that, from year to year throughout her entire life in school, her success depended on whether or not the teacher liked her and she liked the teacher. I asked her, "What kind of grades did you get in elementary school?"

"Each year it varied," she said, "depending on the teacher. One year I would just do terrible, and the next year if she believed in me and I liked her, then I would get B's."

*****

Sally's goal at Nesbitt College was to get a degree in education and become a teacher. She told about negative memories and extreme feelings of inadequacy.

She said she was embarrassed, and she talked about how overwhelming it was. I asked, "And how were you feeling about yourself by that time?"

She thought a minute and then replied: "Confused. Confused and not really knowing what I was going to do with myself and how I would support myself. I didn't know what I was going to do. I just decided that I would have to leave. So after two years, I moved back home."

Sally's voice echoed the despair that she must have felt at that time.

I asked, "Were you thinking you were not smart enough or questioning your ability at that point?"

Sally's reply was, "Yeah, I really didn't know what to do. I didn't know what was wrong with me."

She said she was "terrible" in college English, but she said, ". . . although in freshman year, I received a B in English class, which would be incredible, but I liked the teacher. . . ."

I asked Sally to try to tell me if the teachers she liked had anything in common. She said, "They paid attention to me. They liked me as a person. They paid special attention to me. They believed in me. That is so important."

*****

Sally was convinced that she was terrible at both English and math. She was absolutely convinced that her lack of English skills was her nemesis in college. She said she never should have been accepted into college because of her poor English skills.

At one point, expressing fear about the prospect of returning to college, Sally said, "I couldn't write a term paper to save my soul!"

I tried to reassure her a little by telling her about some support services at the college she talked about attending. She said, "I don't even know if I can do it… I couldn't write a term paper. I haven't got the faintest idea… I don't know."

I said, "I know you're really afraid of term papers."

"I am," Sally said. "My English is extremely poor."

Since I had heard this theme several times, I said, "But you speak very well. You're very, very articulate."

She said, "Everybody tells me that, but I can't put it down on paper."

The thought of returning to college was overwhelming for her. She said, ". . . And math, you might as well forget that. I am terrible at math. I mean awful. I remember taking one elementary math class at Nesbitt and I could not do it." She dragged the words out for emphasis, and continued, "I could not get it. All of my roommates were taking it. I would study right along with them and get it, and then go in and take a test and I flunked…."

Later, referring to the vocational school where she got her medical assistant training, I said, "But, I think maybe you're discounting your Rotman experience a little bit."

"Really?" she asked. I reaffirmed the thought, but she said, "I didn't like it. They had record keeping, and I didn't like that because I also have dyslexia: I invert numbers...."

Sally also talked about another problem. She said, "And my mind, my mind was always racing, but I never wanted to look strange so I always had to be in control and appear very relaxed, so to speak, and don't want to be stared at. I just had to learn that your head is always racing on to the next thing, on to the next, never enjoying the moment. Looking at the clock always; I only have to sit here an hour. If I can sit here for an hour, this will be over, this will pass. I'll be on to the next thing. And feeling that way after only about three or four minutes, it's difficult."

In a later interview, she said she could stay focused only about ten minutes of an hour. Discussing a data-processing class she had taken at the community college after her vocational school experience, but before her diagnosis and treatment for ADD, she said, "It was beyond me; I couldn't stay focused." She said she had more success staying focused at the vocational school because she was more interested in the subject matter.

Sally said she liked lectures, discussions, and paperwork, but she cheated on her labs. She was referring to experiences at the vocational school, where she obtained certification as a medical assistant. However, she referred to the vocational school as "pretend school, not real college." I am not sure she would view her preferred learning styles in "pretend school" and "real college" the same way. In any case, she was the one interviewee from whom I did not obtain a clear indication about learning style preference.

*****

When Sally first went away to the small private college to pursue a teaching degree, she felt she tried all the support services possible and still didn't succeed. She related the following: "I tried having tutors; I tried taking classes over, and I would fail them. And I couldn't do it. I tried a type of, teaching you how to study, that type skill. It was a class, a four-week help type of class, but it didn't help me because I didn't have the background. I couldn't write a term paper. I couldn't try to get twelve years of school in four weeks in a self-help class. It wasn't going to work."

In a second interview, Sally and I were discussing her experiences at the vocational school. When I asked if she used any special accommodations there, she said she never tried them. She didn't say whether or not she knew if they were available.

*****

At the vocational school Sally obtained a certificate as a medical assistant, but she has never reached her original goal of being a teacher. Her decision to abandon that effort was because she "couldn't do the book work."

College was too much pressure for her. She said, "I couldn't do it. I couldn't do it, so I decided after two years that I was spending a lot of money and I wasn't getting anywhere."

She said she had no choice but to leave. I asked her if it was because the college asked her to leave, or if she just knew she wasn't going to make it.

Sally replied, "I knew I wasn't making it and I wasn't going to get better. I had two years into it, and my class would graduate in two years, and I wasn't even close to it. And, not only that, I couldn't do it. And I realized that and it was an awful expensive playtime, so to speak."

Sally talked at length about the struggles she went through during her two years in college. She said: "I really shouldn't have been accepted into college, but they take anybody where I went. And I really shouldn't have been accepted because I found, because of my poor English skills, I could not write a term paper. I found that I was embarrassed, very embarrassed. I just didn't have the skills to do it. So, it made me feel bad."

Sally is exceptionally attractive physically and interpersonally, and she believed that her looks and pleasing personality had carried her along in her younger years. Her experience in college, however, made it clear to her that those things couldn't sustain her in that environment. She left confused and defeated. Even now, 14 years later, she still doesn't believe that she is capable of being successful in college. The impact on her self-esteem was crushing.

Chapter 6

They Made It Through a Bachelor's Degree

Tim

"I guess I'm looking for stimulus, something to keep me interested. In photography, we did a lot of hands-on, which, obviously, I was back in my element, so I did well. In law enforcement we did a lot of hands-on . . . defense tactics, driving, search and seizure, approaching cars, approaching people. You know, a lot of different things they'd have you do, have you practice on."

Versatile and Hyperfocused

Tim was a 39-year-old prison guard and owned his own desktop publishing business at the time of our interviews. Although his initial educational goal was to obtain a university degree in photography, he received an associate's degree in law enforcement and later returned for a bachelor's degree in a nontraditional program for adult students. If he had any learning disability, he was not aware of it. He had been diagnosed with and treated for ADD about two years before I interviewed him. He was uncertain about how his ADD diagnosis related in time to the completion of his bachelor's degree. They had happened at roughly the same time in his life.

Tim had suffered some crushing blows to his self-esteem while he was in college, and he wondered if he was intelligent enough. Although Tim had shown enough academic promise to gain acceptance into a major state university with competitive admissions standards, he started college twice before he finally became motivated to get an associate's degree in law enforcement, and then a bachelor's degree many years later. Tim began at a community college, and he told me, "I went to Capitol Community College because it was the only way they would release me in January from high school. I went there for a while and basically just didn't do well. I got a letter the next spring saying, 'We'd like you to take a term off and see if you'd rather come back or not.' My major at the time was photography, so I tried Overhill State University, and maybe six months later I went down there for a term. Had a great time.... Didn't learn much, didn't do well academically, but had a real good time down there."

"You had a good time. Partying?" I asked.

"Partying, yeah. The dorm I got into was all the art students. They were all heavy partyers at the time, so we all just kind of got caught up in that scene."

Tim told me, ". . .I came back from Overhill, went to CCC again, finished up my associate's, and then ten or twelve years later I went to Silver Springs and got my B.A."

His associate's degree was not in an art-related field; it was in law enforcement. The Silver Springs bachelor's degree was in business. Silver Springs offers a nontraditional course for adults who have associate's degrees; they can get a bachelor's degree by attending class just one night a week.

As we talked about the struggles in his early years of college, Tim said to me, "There were times I would wonder if I was smart enough. You know, if this is something I'm capable of doing. Now, in retrospect, that's a stupid argument, but that's something going through your head: 'Can I do this?'"

He told me about feeling inferior to other students: "Well, they must have something up on me because they're just picking everything right up and I'm struggling like hell and I'm treading water." Obviously Tim found the situation frustrating, and his self-esteem suffered.

Tim told me about the types of instructors to whom he related positively. He said, "The instructors that stayed with me were the ones that were more dynamic, would interact with the class, would ask you questions. So, if they were moving around a lot in the classroom I could keep my attention on them."

Tim thinks the reason he was successful was that he was motivated by a career goal. However, he also said that he thinks one of the reasons he liked law enforcement classes was that they were taught by "ex-cops." He said, "You're always taught by ex-cops and they always have these stories to tell. When they tell stories they get excited and they start moving around the classroom, and that would keep my focus. The guys that came out and stayed in one spot, and get their papers out and start talking, would lose me in a few minutes."

Tim did not volunteer the view that the personalities (attitudes) of instructors influenced his success, but he agreed when I asked him. He definitely knew the types of teacher behavior he liked.

Later in the interview, I said, "I think you told me that you like to write."

Tim replied, "I hate to write, but I have good writing skills."

Later still, we were talking about Tim's expertise with computers. He told me, "What got me started into computers is that I can't spell worth a damn."

"You cannot?" I asked.

"I cannot spell," Tim reaffirmed. "And I think that goes back to spelling means concentration, repetition. And I could never sit and do it. Computers have spell checkers."

It is interesting that Tim's current passion is desktop publishing, a skill he taught himself after being introduced to the wonders that computers could do to assist him with writing and spelling.

Tim also complained of a lack of focus in the classroom. He gave examples which illustrate the problem that so many of the interviewees talked about—falling asleep or daydreaming. Tim said, "I remember trying not to fall asleep a lot. Being bored ... daydreaming a lot, not picking up on the instructor. It was very hard to focus on what he was saying and stay on track with him. This was probably the hardest thing in college or even high school. I'd get one of these guys that wanted to lecture and either I would start falling asleep or I'd start daydreaming or something else would happen. I was a great doodler when I was a kid. I never really stayed on track with what the central focus should have been. I was off in different directions."

*****

Tim said he liked instruction which included visuals. He said, "If they had something that they were showing me, describing you know, pictures . . . I guess I'm looking for stimulus, something to keep me interested." Tim also liked hands-on learning. He said, "In photography, we did a lot of hands-on, which, obviously, I was back in my element, so I did well. In law enforcement we did a lot of hands-on. . . defense tactics, driving, search and seizure, approaching cars, approaching people.

You know, a lot of different things they'd have you do, have you practice on."

Outside the classroom, Tim wanted to be isolated to study. Moreover, Tim didn't see any difference in his preference for an isolated environment either before treatment for ADD or after. When I asked him about his preference, he said, "I had to have complete quiet … I even do now. Like I was working on a newsletter this morning, and I've got to have the radios off, the TVs off, everything off. If the radio is playing, it's going to catch my attention and I'm going to start listening to the song. If the TV is going, I'm going to want to go up there and see what's going on. I've got to be isolated. It's got to be totally quiet. The same thing if I was going to study."

Overall, Tim attributed his success at college to his switch to the law enforcement curriculum, which he found interesting. He said, "It started out in photography, and that's what I went to Overhill State for was photography, and I did so-so there. I was invited not to return for a term so I could figure out which way I'm going, and then I changed over to law enforcement. And that's where I got my associate's—in law enforcement."

A few minutes later he said, " When I came back I switched into a law enforcement curriculum. And for some reason, I seemed to catch fire. My grades were not great, but they came up to around a 3.0, which was far better than I was doing before." And a few minutes after that, he said, "I think going into law enforcement brought everything up. I think I left Capitol Community College with a 3.2 average or something like that."

*****

Tim began his college career majoring in photography, changed his major to law enforcement, and is currently working in two careers: prison guard and desktop publishing. He is not enjoying his law-enforcement-related career currently, but he has worked in that field for fifteen years ("It's not that I'm really enjoying it, but it permits me to do the things I enjoy doing"). He said, "I did corrections work plus law enforcement work, back to corrections work and now I'm working as a prison guard at Homer State Prison for three days a week in 12-hour shifts . . . and doing desktop publishing."

At the time of our interview, Tim was deeply involved in desktop publishing. He told me, " I'll get into manuals about computers or design manuals or things like this and I can get lost in them."

Tim gave examples of becoming hyper-focused on his desktop publishing work. He said, "Last night I got another client with my publishing. So I spent the morning working on getting a presentation for her to show things to her first thing for a newsletter. I was supposed to see Dr. Samson this morning. Well, I got focused over there and everything else was gone. I didn't think about it until she called."

I told him some other people who have ADD speak about getting hyper-focused on some things. He said, "That's what happens. Because like Betty will come home and I'll be working on the computer, and you know the house could blow up around me. And I'll block everything out. It's just like a tunnel. I have tunnel vision right now. And it's a safe world— maybe that might be part of it. It's a good way to describe it. It's hyper-focus. You know, the world blocks out at that point."

Considering how Tim becomes so absorbed in his computer work, it was no surprise to hear him say he finds it rewarding and is successful with it. He said, "The desktop publishing to me is very rewarding when you put something together and like I'm doing all the art work for the newsletter and all the headers. To me that is very rewarding because when I'm done it's there. It's mine and I've done it."

I asked, "And you've become pretty successful at this?"

He replied, "So far it seems to be, yeah. I've got eight solid accounts now, and it looks like it's going to expand."

Overall, Tim has found success and satisfaction in the fields of corrections and desktop publishing.

*****

Tim is uncertain about whether or not he had any college classes after his diagnosis and treatment. If he did the classes were in a nontraditional degree program, which he saw as quite different from "regular" college classes. I asked him, ". . . If you went back now that you've received treatment and are on medication, do you think that anything would be different?"

"I think I'd do better," Tim replied. "I think I'd do a lot better."

"Tell me what 'better' means to you," I asked.

"Well, now I have a better direction of what I want to do, which would help. And I know that I have better concentration level and I'm a lot calmer...."

Tim, also, believes the college experience would be improved by treatment and medication.

Dale

"But I think the Attention Deficit Disorder was probably a very good facilitator of keeping me shy and somewhat withdrawn. I think that once I came to terms with what was going on with me, that I wasn't stupid, or that I wasn't dumb, that there was actually something facilitating this process, then I could say, 'Hey, these are the opportunities I have; now I understand where I'm coming from and what is the proper medication to help me focus.' And it really helped improve my self-esteem."

Slowly and Surely—He Persevered

Dale was a 26-year-old computer technician for a major university at the time of our interviews. His initial educational goal was to obtain a bachelor's degree in music. Instead, he obtained a bachelor's degree in telecommunications. He had attended a community college for three years before transferring to the university. He said he may have been diagnosed with nonspecific learning disabilities during high school, but he was uncertain. His diagnosis for ADD occurred during his community college career, about six years before our interviews. He had been receiving treatment for ADD during most of his college career.

Dale stated directly that an instructor can "make or break" a class. He told several stories of high school teachers who had a direct negative impact on him. Regarding his high school experiences, he said, "I found very few of the classes that I had were really interesting or inspiring. There were a few that, you know, the instructor really made a difference in the class and it was fun to learn."

Dale's main interest in high school was music, and I questioned him about what classes he had taken. He said, "Oh, I played in symphonic orchestra and I played an acoustic bass. And I played in the jazz band as well."

"And you did that throughout high school?" I asked.

Dale replied, "Yep, I played for four years, actually three and a half years, for the orchestra, and then jazz band for one or two, and I quit that primarily just because of the instructor. I didn't feel he had the type of leadership and inspiration qualities that would pull people together, and this type of thing."

Dale was the only interviewee who never dropped out after starting his college work. He began at the community college straight out of high school to embark upon a four-year bachelor's degree program. I am not sure it is accurate to say this was his goal. He didn't really want to go to college then, but he told me his parents made him do it. He said, ". . . I went right in. Of course, against my wishes. I wanted to do the old 'take a year off and try to get focused on what you want to do.'"

*****

Dale disclosed feelings of low self-esteem during high school and the early portions of his college career. Rather early in our first interview, Dale told me, "I have always had very low self-esteem ... it's like, 'How come you can't do this?' It was always, like, 'What's wrong with you?' I knew something. I knew I was different. I always knew I was different as a kid, but I didn't know why. 'What is up with me?' 'Oh, I'm different. I'm not like the others. Something's wrong with me.' And then I got real withdrawn."

I pursued the issue of instructors with Dale. "I'm wondering if the kind of instructors you had made a difference in the courses you selected?"

Dale confirmed my suspicion: "Oh, of course. I think that most people would probably say that in the college experiences an instructor can really make or break a course. They can have the same material. It's like telling a joke. One person can tell a joke one way and have the timing down and, oh, it's hilarious. But the other person can deliver the same lines and it falls on the floor."

Throughout my interviews with him, Dale said that, for the most part, when he enjoyed a class it was because of the instructor. He was emphatic about the negative impact which the unpleasant personality of instructors had on his college career. When he was struggling along at the community college, he flunked two classes because he quit going to class. Ironically, those two classes were music classes, and Dale is gifted in music. His primary interest for most of his life had been music. He could play by ear, and he played in bands from the time he was 15 or 16 years old. Describing one teacher, he said, "The instructor in this case was a real asshole ... was just real negative, a real cynic: 'What do you mean you don't know!' This type of thing. A real attitude."

Dale also attributed failing the other music class to instructor attitude. He said he had been getting about a 3.5 (on a 4.0 scale) in that class when he dropped it to play in a band. The teacher's response, he said, was derogatory: "What are you doing, dropping my class because you're playing in a rock band!" Then the teacher told him to sign a drop form, and Dale thought he would get a withdrawal grade based on his performance so far in the class. When his grades came, he received a failing grade, which he partially attributed to the teacher's attitude.

In a later interview, I asked Dale what advice he would

give to college instructors who knew they would have some ADD students in their classrooms. Part of his response was about instructor personality. He said, "From the classes I've had, there are good instructors and there are poor instructors. There's information and materials that needs to be disseminated, that needs to be taught."

Dale also mentioned that even in lab-based classes he liked the "human element." He didn't like classes in which he thought students were treated like cattle and just pushed along. He definitely thought the personality and attitude of instructors were important to his success.

*****

Much of what Dale said about his lack of focus in the classroom related to his K-12 school experiences rather than his college experiences. He was diagnosed and treated relatively early in his college career, so maybe he didn't experience lack of focus much during college. Possibly my questioning just didn't draw out his memories about college fully. However, regarding school in general, he said, ". . . I had difficulty in concentration or focusing on anything. I didn't know it; I just thought I was just plain lazy." Later, talking about how he hated math, he said, "And I never could keep my concentration on anything. I really tried...."

Dale was the only interviewee who did not complain about falling asleep in class, but he did talk about daydreaming in the classroom and the problems that created. He said, "My attention, you know in terms of listening skills, were pretty poor. I mean, like the instructor would be talking about something, and most of the time I'd end up daydreaming and then caught in the situation: 'Okay, Dale, would you show us how to do this particular problem?' and I didn't know what he was talking about. I've been caught in that position a few times."

Dale also recalled instances when he was supposed to be studying and something else would attract his attention. He would intend to delay just momentarily to be with a friend, read another book or magazine, or listen to some music, but his delays would be more than momentary.

Dale did not go into detail about his learning style preferences, but he did say he had poor listening skills, so I conclude that he prefers the visual. We were discussing the types of classes Dale liked and disliked in college, when he mentioned a certain science class he had taken at the local community college, a class which included activity in an independent learning lab. I said to him, "Somebody else mentioned that very class to me earlier today, about liking it because it gave an opportunity for hands-on. . .more of an experiential learning. "

"The lab, yeah," Dale said. "The physics class was like that, too. But actually, quite honestly, I thought the labs were a pain in the ass."

"Did you?" I asked, somewhat surprised.

Dale continued, "You know, I liked the idea of discovering and so forth, but the way it was presented was, 'Here, go in here and scratch these rocks with a hardness tester, then go over here and ....' So it was, kind of like, I felt like, you know, cattle. 'Come on, move through and finish the project and then move on; next!'"

"How would you have liked it to have been?" I asked.

Dale said, "Having the instructor there, going over the lab and then showing, providing an example, and then after providing an example, having everyone initiate it and going through and doing it.... But I just like the human element interaction when you can have someone there to demonstrate and then you can go through and discover stuff and have that interaction."

Dale seemed to prefer not only the visual, but also an instructor to interact with.

*****

Dale had received special supportive services in elementary school and high school, but did not use them in college. He told me about having a math tutor in high school, and I asked him if he ever used tutoring in college. His response was, "No."

I questioned him further, asking, "Did you ever have a study-techniques class or reading class or anything like that?"

Again, his response was, "No."

One of Dale's main themes was that, as a student with ADD, he did not want to be singled out. He described his feelings of alienation from the other students when he had to leave the classroom to obtain special learning assistance in elementary school. He wouldn't want others to have reason to feel like that. He said, rather sardonically, "I wouldn't feel like I'd want a press release sent to the instructor: 'Hey' (he raised his voice) 'I have a deficiency, so just in case I don't do well on a test it's because I have ADD.'"

Following that discussion, I said to Dale, "I know you didn't use any accommodations because you didn't want to be different, but do you know if there were any accommodations available at the community college or university when you went there to assist you if you had wanted them?"

Dale replied, "Yes, I think there was like a learning resource center. I think most universities have that. I think the community college had that. I never took advantage of it. I didn't feel like I needed it. The classes I was taking I was doing quite well in." My guess is that Dale might not have done quite as well if he had not been diagnosed and treated for ADD relatively early in his college career. Of course, there is no way of knowing whether or not support services could have made a difference.

When Dale responded to the question about study environment, I am fairly certain, he was speaking about his recent college experience, which was while he was taking medication. He prefers some extraneous stimuli; he likes people around when he studies.

Dale said, "I like quiet, but I like to have other people around. When I'm by myself, especially when I'm in my apartment or at my parents' house or something by myself, I'm very easily distracted. It's hard for me to concentrate sometimes studying by myself because I daydream a lot. When I'm in an environment like the library where other people are around studying, it kind of inspires that mind-set. When I'm by myself, I end up going off.... Sometimes I listen to music, but generally that's not a good idea because I end up losing focus."

*****

Dale changed his major at least twice. However, the goal when he began was to get a bachelor's degree, and he never stopped persisting for eight years until this goal was accomplished. Dale's story, as he summed it up, was as follows: "I started attending Covert Community College in the fall of 1986 and was at CCC until 1989. Then, from there I transferred to Midwestern State University. I basically had a variety of different studies, ranging anywhere from, originally what they had called their music block, music curriculum, to media technology. And once I got focused, I ended up transferring to Midwestern State in the telecommunications program. And just graduated actually last May."

Dale accomplished his initial out-of-high-school degree goal without dropping out. However, he took about twice the traditional time to earn a bachelor's degree. He was telling me that he had played in bands and worked all the way through college, and he gave the following example of his typical schedule: "Our band would practice maybe two to four days a week, have gigs at least once a week, sometimes spaced out longer. I would work at least 20 to 25 hours and then take anywhere between 8 and 12 credits, usually 8. I'd take one or two classes...."

I asked him, "I wonder if just taking 8 to 12 credits helped you stay more focused?"

He responded, "It did." He told me about a very stressful experience he had at the university in trying to take more credits than he usually took. Taking it slowly was an asset to Dale.

*****

Dale was struggling through community college when he was diagnosed. He obtained medication and behavioral therapy, and went on to earn a bachelor's degree at a major university.

In our second interview, Dale talked about his employment since graduating from college. The self-esteem issue came up again. "You described yourself as quiet, shy, and withdrawn when you were younger," I recalled.

"Now you have these two jobs since you've been out of college that require pretty high-level people skills. Do you think that your personality has changed or what?" I asked.

"I think I've learned to be more confident in myself," Dale replied. "I think part of my insecurities—I still have insecurities, but I mask them pretty well, or at least try to. But I think the Attention Deficit Disorder was probably a very good facilitator of keeping me shy and somewhat withdrawn. I think that once I came to terms with what was going on with me, that I wasn't stupid, or that I wasn't dumb, that there was actually something facilitating this process, then I could say, 'Hey, these are the opportunities I have; now I understand where I'm coming from and what is the proper medication to help me focus.' And it really helped improve my self-esteem."

Dale was feeling a certain amount of satisfaction in his work. During our second interview, he explained a contrast between him and his siblings. (They had always been very athletic and had become successful in business professions. He was always very musically or creatively inclined, which was not as high in the family's values.) Dale's assessment of his current situation was: "At least at this point in my career I've found something that allows me to express my potential."

Dale is one of the interviewees who were diagnosed relatively early in their college careers. He was in treatment six of the eight years he was working on his degree. When I asked what difference the Ritalin made in his life, he told how it had affected his college career positively.

"What kind of differences did you notice?" I asked.

He replied, "Um, elevation of mood. Most definitely, elevation of mood. Felt good, felt happy.... And I could focus and then get inspired. I mean it made me feel, 'Hey, I feel really good. I'm going to get this done; I'm going to do it.' And I would get it done. And I'd say, 'I did it! I got it done!' Where before, I'd be kind of like, uninspired. But it really provided a platform to allow me to concentrate. Most definitely. I think that it was the catalyst for getting the change. 'Cause I was just, I didn't know what I wanted to do, I was wasting time, taking classes, wasting my parents' money. Finally, I said, you know, 'You get your shit together.' And I said, 'Okay.' I got focused, and if anything, what it did, it put me on the right track and I got focused...."

Dale definitely felt his treatment for ADD made him more successful in college than he had been before.

Chapter 7

Into Postgraduate Professional School

Mike

*"I was taking classes at CCC off and on; I still had the diffi-
culty. After I had seen Dr. Samson and I was placed on the
medication, it made a world of difference, and it did so by
keeping me focused, on task. I found I learned more in less
time, if you will. And part of it was not reading and rereading."*

Into Law School and Hit the Wall

Mike was a 40-year-old sales representative for Intocal Worldwide, a large manufacturing plant. He had completed a
bachelor's degree at a small private college in four years and
attended law school for one year. He had no knowledge of
having any learning disabilities. When I met him, he had been
diagnosed with ADD, and had been receiving treatment for
ten years. His diagnosis and treatment began after he dropped
out of law school, but he had taken some classes at the community college after that.

Mike had intended to be an attorney. He told the story this
way: "I attended college immediately after high school, which
was 1971-75. Studied history, political science and the pre-
law curriculum and graduated from St. John's College.... I
think I really realized I had a problem when I went into law

school. I went one year to Woodrow Law School… and the amount of reading was enormous…. Had I stayed another term, I would have flunked out."

During our first interview, Mike related a story of a math teacher who intimidated him so badly that he took as little math as possible thereafter. "My hardest courses, I think, were math," he said.

"Were they?" I asked.

"Uh huh," Mike replied. "Algebra totally. . . . However, I feel the instructor was intimidating."

"Now, this was college math?" I asked.

"No, this was high school math," Mike clarified. "He was an intimidating figure to me, anyway. And, at that age, I still wasn't into the groove of asking questions or being in front of a class saying, 'I don't understand it,' when everybody else did."

"Sure," I said, expressing understanding.

"So, ultimately, I barely. . . ." Mike broke off and went on, "That was my weakest, and it scared me to death from ever taking any further math class."

"Do you remember what he did to intimidate you?" I asked.

Mike answered, "I think it was his teaching methods more than anything, and maybe just his physical appearance. I know a lot of the girls in the class didn't like him, and some of them even dropped out of the class. He was the football coach . . . and he had that coaching demeanor with him in the class-room…. At that age I was intimidated."

"Do you think you had math trouble before?" I asked.

"No," Mike said without hesitating. "In fact, I did relatively well. I won't say I was an A student, but I was about in the B's."

Other than a modern math class that was required for college graduation, Mike never went near another math class after the teacher/coach experience.

*****

Mike had a lot to say about damage to self-esteem in college. He had sailed through high school fairly easily with a strong positive self-concept. He was an athlete, he did fine academically, and his parents provided a substantial amount of positive reinforcement. Then he went to college, and the story changed.

As an undergraduate, he was aware he had to work longer and harder than other students (especially his roommates). However, his grades were satisfactory and he wasn't greatly concerned about his situation. Then he attended law school for a year. He told me, "As things progressed at Woodrow [law school] and I started finding it harder and harder to even get the C's, that's where I really began to feel defeated. I think that's where I really felt defeated and I didn't know why. I thought, I'm putting in the time; I'm reading it or at least I told myself I'm reading this material. I took the notes; I read; I studied; I did all the things I thought were going to help me, but I was not getting it."

Mike drew me a verbal graph to illustrate what happened to his self-esteem. He said, "If I were to draw a graph, you'd start from kindergarten and obviously you work up and you progress. It probably would have peaked academically somewhere between the twelfth grade and my junior year in college and then you would be looking at a gradual decline."

"Of self-esteem?" I asked.

"Um huh," Mike confirmed.

"Okay," I said. "So, the first few years of college your self-esteem wasn't that bad. But law school really got to be the pits."

"It was the pits! It was extremely the pits!" Mike said emphatically.

Mike told poignant stories about how he would agonize over his studying, spending at least an hour more than his roommates each study session, only to produce less. He said, "I didn't want to fail. I did not want to fail. So I found myself reading and rereading. And sometimes I didn't know if I knew what I just read." He said he was distracted by every movement. If he sat by a window and even if he saw the shadow of a bird that flew by, it distracted him. He said, "I wasn't getting a return on my investment. I mean, if I were a stockbroker, I was a failure. I was not getting a good return on my investment."

*****

Mike, also, mentioned not paying attention in the classroom but covering up for it well. He said, ". . .Well, it wasn't that I was distracted formally. I mean I was doing one of these numbers: looking right at the instructor and he or she probably believed, 'This boy's attentive,' but it was going right through. I mean I wasn't hearing a word they were saying. I was hearing it, but I wasn't grasping it."

Later he explained this behavior further: "I really looked attentive, but I'm watching the second hand on the clock behind you or I'm looking at the fly over there or I'm listening to anything—the clock ticking, the fan running. It could be any number of things. And, like I said, I was good at masking it."

Mike said, "Lecture classes literally would put me to sleep ...." He said he wouldn't look asleep, however, because he's Catholic and his school upbringing taught him to look attentive.

Mike did not express a strong preference for hands-on learning, but he did express a preference for the visual. He mentioned liking classes especially for that reason. When he talked about falling asleep during lectures, he said illustrations helped keep him focused:

"Any time there were classes that, for instance on the blackboard there were illustrations, that would keep my attention.... Also, if I were distracted, I could come back and I had something there to put me right back on track. Where a lecture, if you've lost two or three minutes of his lecture, then try to focus, you've missed it because there is nothing there to bring you up to speed."

Mike also said, "Maybe that's one reason I liked accounting so much, because you could always read your book, but you always had your little problems on your forms. Your paper was set up to do that, and it was systematic and that's why I think I liked it." Mike also mentioned preferences for hands-on and other visual experiences in the training for his current job.

*****

Mike never used any support services in college or law school. When I asked him if they had been available, he said: "I know there was tutoring, which I never took advantage of. And, I guess I was just like one of these people, for whatever reason, 'I don't have a problem.' I knew I did, but I wanted to deny it. And I didn't want to admit that maybe I'm not quite as smart as these guys. That was kind of my approach more than anything. I hid it."

Mike said he preferred background noise when he was studying, both before and after treatment with medication. The one difference that he has observed about himself is that he preferred louder music when he was younger and undiagnosed. He said, "You know, my mother used to ask me, 'How can you study with that loud music?' And right now I could not do that like I used to. But I think that loud music was a cover for all the outside distractions. Sitting in a quiet room where you could hear chairs squeak or if you were in a library for instance, without the meds, I was in a position to hear the squeaky chair or to hear the guy in the next study carrel turn a page. It was amazing the little things that would take my focus away from what I was reading…. You know, my mother couldn't understand it. And now, I'm not sure I could do that. I mean, when I do read, whether it's academic or the newspaper, I can have the TV on or the music, but it's not loud; it's kind of a background. Where then, it was loud. And it was kind of designed to put me in my own world, which it did to some extent. Because I wasn't hearing the lawn mower or the shouting in the dorm or two down or wherever it may be."

*****

After the one year in law school, Mike began working in the paint department of an automobile assembly plant. That was fifteen years before I interviewed him. When I asked Mike about his current occupation, he said, "I am a sales rep for Intocal Worldwide. Originally, I started as the training representative there, and I handled technical training…."

When I asked him how he had reached this point in his career, he told me, "I had fifteen years in, August seventh… I started off on the assembly line… I tried different things, and

I knew I didn't want to do that kind of work."

In our first interview, I had asked him if he ever thought about going back to law school. He said, "I'm not sure I would be happy…. I've got a good job, I've got possibilities for advancement within Intocal …."

Also during that interview he told me, "… I don't know for sure, but I believe this, if you were to talk to anyone I've ever worked for, they would say I was a good employee as far as attitude and production and things like that in anything I've done."

If those positive statements are not enough to convince us of Mike's success in a field outside of law, this question and response should confirm it. I said, "You like what you're doing now, don't you?"

He said, "I love it!"

He expressed a similar sentiment the second time I interviewed him, when he was reflecting on the fact that he didn't complete law school and become an attorney. He said, "I was disappointed, but looking back or saying would I be happier, no, and I think a lot of that is I have a job I enjoy; I have a family; I have a wife. I see a future in a new home and advancement in my present job. I have absolutely no remorse or regrets for the way things turned out."

There is no doubt that Mike has found success and satisfaction in his career, which is not in the same field he began to prepare for in college.

*****

With his self-esteem at an all-time low, Mike had dropped out of law school. Soon afterwards he got diagnosed and began treatment for ADD. His diagnosis was approximately 10 years before my interviews with him. Since diagnosis and treatment, he has been very successful in some classes at the local community college. These successes, he says, have renewed his self-esteem.

Reflecting on all this, Mike said, "I'm convinced that, had I not had it stopped right after law school, I'd be a sour old man."

When he was telling me about how easily distracted he had been in classrooms, he reflected on the difference treatment had made for him. He said, ". . . I was taking classes at CCC off and on; I still had the difficulty. After I had seen Dr. Samson and I was placed on the medication, it made a world of difference, and it did so by keeping me focused, on task. I found I learned more in less time, if you will. And part of it was not reading and rereading."

I asked Mike how he thought his earlier undergraduate experience might have been different if he had been diagnosed and treated at that time. He said he thought it would have improved his self-esteem. He explained it this way: "I think I would have the self-esteem. I wouldn't have the loss of self-esteem or at least the deterioration of it, the gradual deterioration, that I experienced. I would also be more apt to seek out the assistance of the people around me, whether it be my roommates, instructors, or whatever."

Later, I posed the question to Mike more directly. I asked, "Do you feel you could be more successful if you went back to college after your diagnosis and treatment?"

He responded emphatically, "Oh, I know I would. I would bet everything I own on it!"

I probed further. "Tell me more about that," I said.

Mike responded, "In my mind and, in fact, I feel that I've proven it substantially (since I've seen Dr. Samson) in my college classes and in the classes that I've got that are work-related. I'm more apt to participate; I'm more apt to stay on-task when you have projects. I know I participate more; there is no doubt in my mind. I know that if I started today in any program, I would do better."

Mike certainly feels strongly that he did better in college after his diagnosis and treatment for ADD.

Kathy

"I went down and talked with the assistant director down at the Southfield campus, and she put me in with a counselor .... I worked with someone over in Handicapper Services and actually went back and did second-grade phonics."

Against All Odds: Medical School

Kathy was a 41-year-old student in her third year of medical school during our interviews. She was in her first year of medical school when she was diagnosed with learning disabilities and ADD. She had received treatment for ADD, and had continued in school for almost two years preceding our interviews.

Like some of the other interviewees, Kathy felt "different" most of her life. She told me, "I can remember being in high school and I really felt like everybody else walked around and knew what they were doing all the time and I always felt like I was in a fog." She rarely felt like she fit in with classmates, and often felt ostracized.

She began her college education in small private colleges working toward a bachelor's degree. She said, "I went from

September to December at Anderson, and then in January I started at Alward. I only went like three or four weeks and had such a tough time. It was like one comedy of errors after another."

I interrupted: "This was just after you were out of high school, like when you were 18 or 19 years old?"

"Yeah, yeah," she continued. "I turned up being pregnant and I had the flu and I mean I had the flu, and then there was a storm and then I found out that I was pregnant, and I was just like, 'Enough is enough, the die is cast and this isn't yielding me anything!'"

Kathy dropped out of college. Fourteen years later, after having six children, she began classes at Deerfield Community College in her hometown. She spent two and a half years at Deerfield getting an associate's degree; then she went to Southfield State University and took three years to get a bachelor's degree with a double major. At the time of our interviews, she was in medical school at Midwestern State University.

*****

Kathy and I were talking about the multiple reasons she had dropped out of college when she said to me, "I think I'd also begun to hit maybe a little bit of a stone wall, because I took a psych class and we were doing some stuff that was hard for me to do and I think I felt one more time some of the ostracism that I couldn't keep up with everyone else in doing some things. And that was just another subtle little thing of, 'Okay, you don't have to do this.'"

"So the fact that you felt different from other people motivated you to quit because you didn't have to do it?" I asked.

"Well, it was just one more thing on top of everything else,"

Kathy replied.

Low self-esteem, resulting in part from her feelings of being ostracized and inadequate, apparently was one of the reasons Kathy dropped out of college. Kathy also mentioned a poor return on her investment when I asked how ADD had affected her academic life. She said she had difficulties with "staying on task." I could hear the frustration in her voice when she said, "I did spend a tremendous amount of effort making myself stay on task, and I just assumed that that was the way everybody was."

Kathy was somewhat contradictory in her responses about whether or not instructors make a difference. When I asked her if she felt that the personality or attitudes of instructors had anything to do with her performance, she said no. She said, "In medical school you are just a number." But I believe that she was focusing on her current instructors. In a later interview she went into some detail about a physician who had been one of her instructors the previous summer. Kathy said he was really good because he was a "down to earth" person. Additionally, she mentioned she was really looking forward to having another instructor who had a similar reputation. So Kathy sees no relation between her success and the personality of her instructors, but she does enjoy the classes of some teachers more than those of others.

Kathy had recently undergone a complete series of tests and was well apprised of her basic skills levels. She was weak in verbal skills, and she knew it.

"One of the most difficult things that I find to do is composing," Kathy told me. "And that will probably never be easy for me. My vocabulary is—I had it tested—I think it was about a seventh-grade level. I swear I'm going to keep records that a street person could read because I don't know if I'll ever be comfortable with all those Latin words and that kind of crap."

Kathy had a lot to say about her lack of focus in the classroom. She said she didn't notice it so much as an undergraduate, but when she got to medical school, it became very apparent. She said, "I did experience some difficulty during my first year before diagnosis; I had begun to experience some difficulty in being able to really tune everything out.... My attention wanders really bad when I listen to lectures. I really have a hard time with that." She also gave a specific example of what happens to her in the clinical portion of her training; she said, "People start talking and it's like the words run together, and there are times when I can just feel myself fade right out and come back. And I say, 'Okay, now, what are they talking about?'"

Kathy said, "The second year it was really bad; sometimes I'd sleep through fifteen minutes of an hour lecture."

Kathy knows she is a visual learner; psychological testing to diagnose her learning disability disclosed an auditory processing deficit. Kathy explained to me, "I think I have always kind of noticed it, but it really became apparent in anatomy class, and that really threw me the first quarter because people would be talking to me, be rambling off these long words and everything, and they'd be two or more questions on down the road and I'd be still deciphering and putting together what that question was."

Later, she said, "I think I used my visual a lot." Apparently, she did; she was in her third year of medical school.

*****

Kathy had used just about every special support service imaginable. She used tutoring, counseling, an MCAT preparation course, phonics instruction at Handicapper Services, extended time limitations, and support from a special services assistant in the medical school. In seeking special support services, she is atypical among the individuals I interviewed for the study.

Kathy took special preparation courses when they were available to her. Before she took her MCAT exam for admission into medical school, she spent eight weeks preparing for it in a summer class on campus. Then, after acceptance but before beginning medical school, she attended another special preparation course to give her a head start.

During Kathy's first year in medical school, she was doing poorly in her classes and was diagnosed with a learning disability. This sparked a mild depression, and she sought assistance. She told me, ". . . I went down and talked with the assistant director down at the Southfield campus, and she put me in with a counselor. I began to do some work with a Ph.D. at the Southfield campus."

Kathy also told me of other support services she sought and used. She said, "I went to teachers sometimes if I needed a little bit extra, to get a little bit of something extra on the side if I needed it.... I worked with someone over in Handicapper Services and actually went back and did second-grade phonics."

During her second year of medical school, Kathy again had trouble and thought about quitting. Again, she went to the assistant director. This time the administrator referred her to someone for special assistance. Kathy said, "And at that time she hooked me up with someone at Southfield who does a lot of tutoring with students, and second semester was much better for me, much better."

This special tutoring assistant in the medical school has been extremely beneficial to Kathy. The person was doing some consulting out of the country at the time of my second interview with Kathy, and Kathy told me, "When she comes back, I'll live in her lap." Obviously, Kathy will go to any length to seek support services and to be successful.

When I first asked Kathy about her best study environment, she told me that when she started college she couldn't study at home, but would go to the community college cafeteria to study. Believing I grasped her main point, but checking, I said, ". . . I want to make sure I heard you clearly: your best study environment is to completely isolate yourself?"

Her response surprised me: "Yes, but in a very busy environment. Because when I went from community college to Southfield, it took me awhile because I didn't find that it worked well in the library because everybody was quiet.... And what I ended up doing was, I had a restaurant where I'd go sit with a pot of coffee and the restaurant noise was the background noise, but I was focused on what I was doing, and that was what really centered down for me."

"So there has to be some background noise?" I asked.

"Yeah," she said. "And it's not a TV; it's not music or anything like that. It's people noise, but noise that I don't have to think about, that really is not part of me, and I don't have to respond to in any way."

She told me that she had never used music much as noise to study by, that she didn't think the radio was quite "where it's at" for her. Summing up, she said, "I do know that I use that background as a way of, I don't know, walling myself off and really being able to concentrate."

Kathy, also, has taken her course of study slowly, and she interrupted it by dropping out. In fact, she didn't make a really good start until fourteen years after she graduated from high school. Then she took plenty of time completing associate's and bachelor's degrees. She also opted to extend the first two years of medical school into three years. Of this, she said, "I went into Thanksgiving break saying, 'I'm going to quit.' And they're like, 'extend, extend.' . . . . And I was like, 'Okay.' So I extended, and it backed off my load tremendously." She explained further: "Medical school is going to take me five years because I extended during the first two years, which is one of the options that they give you there at Midwestern State University." Kathy, like Dale, took lighter loads as a way to deal with some of the problems college presented.

*****

Kathy was still in college at the time of the interviews, so her career success could not be measured. It is clear, however, that she is on the road to successfully completing medical school, a goal she did not have when she first began college, right after high school. She told me about making her career decision when she went back to school after a fourteen-year lapse. During her first year, she told me, she had a 3.75 grade point average, and then she spent the next summer thinking about what she wanted to do. She said, "And it was at that point that I kind of set my sights on becoming a doctor.... And, so, that was kind of it, and I had a marvelous counselor at Deerfield. So when I decided I wanted to be pre-med, the counselor, he was a marvelous man, he didn't look at my age as a deterrent ...." A few minutes later, she shared with me some of the success she has experienced in that academic decision: " I graduated with a double major. And I graduated cum laude."

Kathy reflected back to her motivation during her undergraduate days. She said, "I just dug my heels in so hard that when I got to school, I was going to do it, by hook or by crook.

Whatever it took, I was going to do it." Her determined use of support services demonstrates that she did, in fact, do whatever it took. She went on to medical school and, at the time of our interviews, she was in her third year. It would be premature to say that she is successful and satisfied with her occupation, but she certainly has been successful in the academic preparation for it.

Kathy was the other interviewee in this study who was diagnosed while she was still in college. She was in her first year of medical school at the time. I asked her, "After you were diagnosed and got on Ritalin, did you see differences then in your performance in school?"

"Yes," Kathy replied, "from the standpoint that I could stay on-task longer. I could get a little bit more out of studying ... stay on studying a little bit longer."

Kathy also felt that the psychotherapy she had as part of her treatment helped her with self-management in group dynamics in her classes. She told me, "I did a lot of work with Dr. Samson about handling disruptiveness, as far as being in a group. . . impulsiveness in talking in a group, impulsiveness to just butt in. I was not truly aware of what I was doing until I started to address just what ADD meant."

Another benefit to Kathy from her diagnosis was that she gained the option of requesting individual testing, with unlimited time, rather than taking her tests with a whole group. She described how that was helpful to her: ". . . and then, when I got the diagnosis, the one thing they offered me was I can take my tests by myself. I have unlimited time. And I thought, 'I don't need that.' Well, I've been through two tests now, and I've gone to them and said, 'This is the way I want it to be.' During this past year, taking the tests by myself, that has begun to be the way I function the best.... Some of it is that I can sit there and read questions out loud to myself, less distract-ibility. I don't have to be worried about tuning out everybody else."

Kathy definitely thought there would have been positive differences had she been diagnosed and treated before her bachelor's degree.

Chapter 8

What Their Stories Tell Us

In some ways the experiences these seven individuals related to me were vastly different; in other ways they were similar. First, it became apparent that many of them experienced difficulty in college. For the majority, prior academic difficulties and the symptoms of ADD led to a lack of confidence in their ability to succeed. Many felt their performance in school was often influenced by their instructors' personality or attitude towards them. Several credited their success in difficult courses to understanding teachers who were willing to provide them with encouragement and extra help. They struggled to make it through, citing problems with inattention and lack of focus, difficulties with English and math. Most, unfortunately, did not take advantage of student support services on campus to assist them while going to school. All but one of them agreed that had they been diagnosed and treated for their ADD while in school, their chances for success would have been greater. Excerpts from my interviews with these individuals, found in the past three chapters, hopefully have provided a better understanding of the frustrations, challenges, and opportunities that students with ADD may face in college.

Emotional Reactions

Diminished Self-Esteem

One of the most striking findings from the data collected

through interviewing these seven adults with ADD, was that almost all of them were affected emotionally by college as a result of their inability to succeed up to their expectations. With only one exception, they all had had problems with self-esteem throughout their lives and their struggles in college only made them feel worse.

Finding the Right Instructor

Like many students, most of the adults with ADD whom I interviewed felt that the personality (attitude) of their instructors had an influence on their success in the classroom. Finding the right instructor with whom to take a class may mean the difference between success and failure for many students, especially those with disabilities. Instructors who are able to present subject matter in an entertaining, motivating way which captures the attention of the student with ADD can help those with attentional weaknesses focus longer. Teachers who show an interest in the learning needs of their students may be more apt to make accommodations in class to help those who need them. Instructors who are willing to take the time to explain things in different ways or to offer extra help can make a substantial difference.

Perceptions of Learning

Weaknesses in English or Math

Most of the individuals with ADD in this study said they believe they have serious inadequacies in English or math or both. For the most part, these observations are their own (except where noted in their stories) and are not substantiated by standardized test results. The observations were unsolicited. There was no question in the interview plan about their performance in any specific course of study. Two interviewees mentioned inadequacies in English, three of them mentioned weaknesses in math, and one mentioned weaknesses in both areas.

Hands-On, Visual Learners
Most of the interviewees in this study said they are visual learners and they prefer hands-on instruction over lectures. Many of them reported falling asleep during lectures. One of the interviewees was unclear about her preference, but the other six definitely stated a preference for visual, or even hands-on, learning. Three of them said specifically that they preferred hands-on learning activities.

Lack of Focus
Not surprisingly, there was one experience which all of the interviewees reported resoundingly. They all talked about lack of focus, all of them in the classroom, and some while studying as well. All seven of them said they fell asleep or daydreamed in classes and four of them had difficulty focusing while they were studying.

How They Dealt with Their Experiences

Seeking Support Services
Many colleges and universities, if not all, currently offer support services for students with special needs. This might or might not have been true when and where these individuals obtained their educations. However, it is true that most of them did not use special support services. Four of them didn't seek out the services, or didn't want to use them. One individual said support services didn't exist at the university he attended (my guess is that maybe services existed, but he was unaware

of them). One individual said she tried some support services and they didn't work. She later went to a vocational school and said she never used support services there. Only one of these individuals, a definite exception, used support services extensively in college. She sought out and used every possible mechanism she could to enhance her success.

It is interesting that Kathy, the person who has achieved the highest degree of academic success among those seven people interviewed, is also the individual who has sought out and used the most support services. Most of the other individuals did not show the interest in support services and did not want to use them, did not think they needed them, or did not think any existed. It is difficult not to wonder about cause and effect in these cases.

Study Environment
The majority of these individuals with ADD preferred a study environment that was not completely quiet and isolated, at least before they were diagnosed and treated. For some of them, being on medication made a difference in how much background noise they preferred. After diagnosis and treatment, they seemed to want less background noise, but still some. Two individuals, however, definitely wanted complete silence and isolation for studying. The seventh interviewee did not provide information about her favored study environment in college.

Larger Reactions and Outcomes

Changed Original Plan
A larger reaction to their college experiences by the individu-

als in this study was to change their original plan. All of them changed their plan in one way or another. They either extended their completion time, some of them leaving school temporarily and returning later, or they left school altogether. One individual consistently persevered and accomplished an original goal. However, that goal, a bachelor's degree, took him eight years to complete. Two participants dropped out of their bachelor's degree programs, but returned several years later to complete their degrees. Four dropped out of the degree programs they were pursuing and have not returned.

Success and Satisfaction Outside Initial College Program
One of the outcomes for these individuals is that most of them have found success or satisfaction in their careers. However, most of them are not in fields that require the college program they first pursued. All five of the males in the study have found a certain degree of success in their careers. All of them have found satisfaction at one time or another, but two of them were beginning to get somewhat frustrated or bored at the time I interviewed them. One of the women was still in college (medical school) at the time of the interviews, so her career success could only be measured in terms of academic success. The seventh individual, the other woman, was an exception in that she had not found success or satisfaction.

College After Diagnosis
Most of the interviewees in this study felt they could be/were more successful if/when they went back to college after diagnosis. Three of them had not taken any college courses after they were diagnosed with ADD. Of these three, two felt they would be more successful if they went back; the third, an exception, did not share their confidence. Two other interviewees

had completed most of their college classes before diagnosis and treatment, but they have taken some classes since and feel they have done better. Another two of the interviewees were actively pursuing their college degrees at the time of their diagnosis and treatment. Both of these individuals felt they did better after treatment. Six of the interviewees definitely felt that the treatment they received for ADD would/did enhance their college success.

Summary

Educators concerned with maximizing the potential of their ADD students will want to remember the emotional reactions and coping mechanisms of these seven individuals. Any college student with ADD can find encouragement in those outcomes and convictions.

The seven individuals whose stories appear in this book might not seem to be different from the average student. Many students with ADD do not seem "different." But these seven are less average than they may first appear. Taken individually, many characteristics listed as symptoms of inattention and impulsivity can be seen in many, if not most, people. A clinical diagnosis of ADD is based on the combination and intensity of these characteristics. Individuals with ADD are clinically more inattentive and impulsive than is developmentally appropriate. This is what makes them different from the average student.

The adults who were interviewed in this study all have ADD, but we cannot use their experiences to generalize about all college students with ADD. The purpose of the study was to describe and analyze the college experiences of these seven adults and the ways they dealt with them. If you can relate to some of these experiences, you can learn from whatever applies to you. The patterns which emerged from the college experiences of these interviewees were as follows:

Emotional Reactions

- College experiences before the individuals were diagnosed often contributed to a diminishing of their self-esteem.
- Most of them felt that the personality (attitude) of their instructors had an influence on their success in the classroom.

Perceptions of Learning

- Most of them felt they had serious inadequacies in English or math or both.
- They all resoundingly experienced a lack of focus in the classroom and/or while studying.
- Most of them said they are visual learners and prefer hands-on instruction over lectures.

Day-to-Day Support

- They usually did not seek out support services—or they thought they did not exist.
- Before they were diagnosed and treated, many of them preferred a study environment that was not completely quiet and isolated; some of them still had that preference after treatment.

Larger Reactions and Outcomes

- They changed their original plans.
- Most of them have found success and satisfaction in

their careers; however, most of them are not in fields requiring the college program they first pursued.

• Most of them felt they could be/were more successful if/when they went back to college after diagnosis.

There is much to learn from the college experiences of the seven individuals portrayed in this book. Two thoughts particularly stand out. One is a consensus view of the interviewees: for students with ADD, college can be a much more successful experience with appropriate diagnosis and treatment. The other thought is suggested by the experience of the interviewee who has been most successful academically, the medical student: special services and accommodations for students with ADD can be vital for success.

The suggestions which follow in the next two chapters are strategies which could contribute to a positive experience for college students who have ADD, especially if their experiences are like some of those described in this book. Chapter 11 is directed at counselors and educators who work with college students with ADD and wish to enhance their students' chances for success.

Chapter 9

Implications for College Students with ADD

If you are a college student with ADD, the themes which emerged in the stories related in this book have many implications for you. The seven individuals whose experiences have been described in this book do not necessarily represent all college students with ADD. However, the patterns in their experiences, along with what we know about the disorder, imply some suggestions for students.

As a college student with ADD, you need to take responsibility for empowering yourself. You will become empowered if you self-advocate and structure your environment, keeping in mind what was learned from the individuals in Chapters 5-7. You need to pay attention to your emotional reactions, enhance learning experiences, and maintain hope and a positive attitude. This chapter will describe tactics you might employ as you assume these responsibilities. Chapter 10 will discuss some specific study skills that may help you to succeed in college. (Please refer as well to Appendix A, *ADD Students' TIPS.*)

Empowerment through Self-Advocacy

Although college students with ADD may frequently rely on help from others (including educators, health care professionals, friends, and family), they also need to be empowered to help themselves. Empowerment is a process in which a person recognizes personal power and ability to gain mastery over their environment. Once empowered, students with ADD will seek ways to advocate for themselves and to structure their environment to help maximize their chances for success.

Students at the postsecondary level must rely heavily on self-advocacy to obtain appropriate programs and services. Students must identify themselves to the appropriate office at the college or university in order to be considered eligible for accommodations. After establishing such eligibility, the student should work closely with this office to determine what programs, services and accommodations the student may need. The back-up of a supportive student services office can be very important.

Self-advocacy often takes the form of requesting accommodations within the learning environment to meet your needs. Accommodations are modifications or adjustments made in normal procedures to assist those with disabilities. When we think of the kinds of adjustments that are made for people with disabilities, what often come to mind are modifications or additions to physical structures to help the physically disabled (e.g., ramps for wheel chairs, electronic doors, reserved parking spaces, etc.). We are not as used to thinking about adjustments that can be made in classrooms to benefit those who have other, less visible impairments such as learning disabilities and attention deficit disorders. Yet, accommodations can also be extremely important for people with these types of disabilities. These accommodations may be such things as extended time for tests, an isolated test-taking environment, and permission to tape-record lectures. Colleges are used to making such accommodations and usually have an office of disability services or some other office to meet the needs of students with disabilities.

Karen Selkowitz (1993) is an excellent example of a student who advocated for herself and structured her environment.

> I re-entered college this past fall. I took three courses, receiving three A's. I worked hard but there were things available to me that made the difference. I use support services at school. This means if I need a notetaker or tutor, the school provides them. I also hand my professors a letter that introduces me as a student with a learning difference explaining how I learn. I break larger tasks into smaller ones… I am able to obtain my textbooks on tape to help me retain information. I read along with my textbooks and listen to the taped book at the same time. When appropriate, I ask my professors for any visual aids that might help me better understand the materials. I sometimes use rhymes or songs to train my memory. With permission from my professor, I tape lectures so that I can fill in the blanks of my notes after class. Color coding my notes and textbook helps keep me organized. (p. 2)

Like Karen Selkowitz, college students with ADD can become empowered to help themselves. They can learn to take initiative in seeing to it that their educational needs are met. Often there is a special campus office to assist them.

Pay Attention to Your Emotional Reactions

Poor self-esteem and school failure are common in people with ADD. It is not surprising, then, that the individuals in this book described themselves as having low self-esteem and said the personalities (attitudes) of instructors had an influence on their success. Other emotional reactions, also, often coexist with ADD. Depression and anxiety are examples. When we consider that individuals with ADD characteristically are academic underachievers, we can understand why college might further diminish their self-esteem and might exacerbate other negative emotions.

Choose the Right College

The first thing you can do to enhance your emotional reactions to college is to select an appropriate school. Among the many variables most people consider when selecting a college are: size of the school, location, tuition costs, living expenses, course offerings, social and political atmosphere, coed or single-gender, athletics, campus activities, etc. There is no research to advise us as to what type of college may be best for students with ADD. Students with ADD can succeed in a wide variety of colleges and universities if they have the ability, preparation, desire, and opportunity to do so.

Common sense suggests, however, that it is important to select a college that is large enough to appeal to your interests and small enough to meet your needs. Large institutions have diverse class offerings, a wide array of extracurricular activities, terrific athletic programs, etc. that can be very attractive. While smaller colleges may lack such diversity, they sometimes can more easily meet the individual needs of their students. This can be vitally important for students who have a disability which will require special accommodations and services.

In choosing a school, if you have ADD, or any other disability, you may also want to consider the range of services offered on campus for students with disabilities. While federal law requires that schools provide assistance for students with disabilities, colleges are not required to maintain a separate student disability services office. Frequently, such services are handled through a Dean of Students Office, with varying success. Depending upon the severity of students' conditions and other factors, the need for assistance and accommodations in school will vary for students with ADD. While not everyone with ADD will require such assistance, for those who do, it is important that the school has the staff, knowledge and procedures in place to help. Therefore, for some, it may be preferable to choose a college with a strong student disability services office, which has counselors who are knowledgeable about a wide range of disabilities and especially about ADD.

It would be a good idea to schedule an interview with an admissions counselor and try to get an understanding of how the school has helped students with ADD in the past, what procedures are followed, and how responsive the faculty has been in accommodating students with special needs. Richard (1992) suggests you should be prepared to ask specific questions, such as these:

- Does the college have an office of student disability services?
- Are there counselors and advisors at the college who are familiar with ADD?
- What documentation does a student need to verify his/ her disability?
- Are students with disabilities, including ADD, given any special consideration during the admission process?
- What specific programs and services are available to students with disabilities?
- Can students with disabilities take a lighter course load

and still be considered full-time students?
- Are faculty fully willing to provide appropriate accommodations and to be available to students with disabilities?

If the admissions counselor is not prepared to answer some of your questions, you could ask to be referred to another appropriate office.

Maintain Strength and Support

To improve your emotional reactions to college, you should:
- Be sure to have a complete treatment plan in place: medication, counseling, and education about ADD.
  - Make arrangements with your medical doctor to refer you to a physician who is closer to you geographically, or to get your medication prescriptions to you in a timely manner.
  - Find a counselor/therapist who is knowledgeable about ADD.
  - Continue to educate yourself about the effects of ADD through books, tapes, speakers, and support groups.
- Establish realistic goals for yourself (perhaps with the help of parents, academic advisors, and/or counselors).
- Work with the student disability services office or a counselor to seek out instructors who have a reputation for being accommodating to students with disabilities.
- Develop a supportive relationship with a counselor at the college, or a therapist in the community, who understands ADD.
- Talk about problems with appropriate persons (e.g., friends, parents, residence hall staff, counselor, clergy).
- Participate in extracurricular activities (e.g., athletics, clubs, sororities or fraternities) which you enjoy and

which utilize your personal strengths.
- Participate in an ADD support group, if one is available, or ask for help in organizing one.
- Constructively celebrate small successes.
- Attend to your physical well-being: exercise, eat nutritionally, and get the appropriate amount of sleep.
- Attend to your spiritual well-being (spend time getting in tune with your "highest self," or with whatever is important to you personally, even if that means just sitting quietly for a few minutes each day becoming centered on your priorities).

Enhance Learning Experiences

The individuals in this book described various possible barriers to their learning. Most of them believed they had serious inadequacies in English or math, or both. They reported a lack of focus—all of them in the classroom, and some while studying as well. Most of them said they are visual learners and prefer hands-on instruction over lectures. Most of them did not seek out special support services. Additionally, although they needed to be free of distractions, many of them preferred a study environment that was not completely quiet and isolated. These findings are not surprising in light of what we know about ADD. However, all these issues can be effectively addressed with knowledge and appropriate strategies.

Knowledge of the Laws

Having ADD is no picnic. It can be a serious disability, and therefore you may be entitled to some protections under the law. When ADD significantly impairs educational performance or learning, individuals with ADD are classified as students with disabilities, or handicaps, under federal law. This was made clear in a "Policy Clarification Memorandum" issued jointly by three federal agencies on September 16, 1991 (CHADD, 1993a).

An important part of being empowered to help yourself is having a thorough knowledge of the federal laws which protect students with disabilities. Laws were enacted to best ensure that students with disabilities are competing on an equal playing field with other students in college who are not disabled.

Section 504 of the Rehabilitation Act of 1973 (RA) and the Americans with Disabilities Act (ADA) were enacted to protect persons with disabilities from discrimination. The Department of Education's Code of Federal Regulations for Section 504 of the Rehabilitation Act states that:

> No qualified handicapped person shall, solely on the basis of handicap, be excluded from participation in, be denied the benefits of, or otherwise be subjected to discrimination under any program which receives or benefits from Federal financial assistance. (34 CFR § 104.4 [a])

This requires that colleges and universities provide equal opportunity in admissions, housing, financial aid, non-academic services and academic/general services.

Regulations for the Rehabilitation Act of 1973 also provide for academic adjustments that might be needed:

> (a) *Academic requirements.* A recipient to which this subpart applies shall make such modifications to its academic requirements as are necessary to ensure that such requirements do not discriminate or have the effect of discriminating, on the basis of handicap, against a qualified handicapped applicant or student .... Modifications may include changes in the length of time permit-

ted for the completion of degree requirements, substitution of specific courses required for the completion of degree requirements, and adaptation of the manner in which specific courses are conducted. (34 CFR § 104.44 [a])

Furthermore, as a general rule and as nearly as possible, evaluations must measure student academic achievement rather than a student's disability. The only exceptions are tests intended to measure skills which may be impaired by the disability. In this regard the Department of Education regulation which implements the Rehabilitation Act states:

> (c) *Course examinations.* In its course examinations or other procedures for evaluating students' academic achievement in its program, a recipient to which this subpart applies shall provide such methods for evaluating the achievement of students who have a handicap that impairs sensory, manual, or speaking skills as will best ensure that the results of the evaluation represents the student's achievement in the course, rather than reflecting the student's impaired sensory, manual, or speaking skills (except where such skills are the factors that the test purports to measure). (34 CFR § 104.44 [c])

Additionally, the college or university must ensure that auxiliary aids are made available to the student who is disabled:

> (d) *Auxiliary aids.* (1) A recipient to which this subpart applies shall take such steps as are necessary to ensure that no handicapped student is denied the benefits of, excluded from participation in, or otherwise subjected to discrimination under the education program or activity operated by the recipient because of the absence of educational auxiliary aids for students with impaired sensory, manual, or speaking skills.

(2) Auxiliary aids may include taped texts, interpreters or other effective methods of making orally delivered materials available to students with hearing impairments, readers in libraries for students with visual impairments, classroom equipment adapted for use by students with manual impairments, and other similar services and actions. Recipients need not provide attendants, individually prescribed devices, readers for personal use or study, or other devices or services of a personal nature. (34 CFR § 104.44 [d])

In July, 1990, The Americans with Disabilities Act (ADA) was passed to end discrimination against individuals with disabilities. It applies to areas of employment, public entities (including public education facilities), and public accommodations (including private education facilities). ADA reinforces protections of the Rehabilitation Act of 1973 and extends them to public and private institutions, including most colleges, even if they do not receive federal assistance (Latham and Latham, 1994a).

To make the best use of 504 and ADA regulations, you must make your disability known to others and ask for special assistance. Obviously, this is a difficult step to take for most college students. Nobody likes to feel different or wants to be treated in any special way unless it is absolutely necessary. Many people with disabilities try quite hard to rely on their own resources to accomplish tasks. However, assistance is sometimes necessary and it is important that students with disabilities learn how to advocate for themselves to obtain what they need.

It is particularly important to seek the assistance of, and to work with, a special student disabilities services office or whatever office may serve the needs of students with disabilities.

Such an office can collect the necessary documentation of your diagnosis, assure you are given maximum privacy and protection, and coordinate any appropriate accommodations.

Strategies for Enhancing Learning

Although many individuals with ADD (some with learning disabilities) have trouble in college, many can be successful if they use appropriate strategies. Many of the strategies suggested earlier to improve a student's emotional reactions to college experiences have a "ripple effect" and will enhance learning as well. These include things you can do before the semester begins, as the semester progresses, and throughout your college experience.

Before the Semester Begins

As you prepare to begin college, you can enhance your chances for academic success if you:

- Know as much as possible about your individual limitations and what accommodations work for you.
- Obtain career counseling from a counselor familiar with your disability. Set goals which are realistic and which motivate you to achieve.
- Arrange to live in a single dormitory room or apartment.
- Obtain records of your disability and share them with the disability services office on your campus.
- Request assistance from the disability services office with:
  - Priority registration.
  - Course substitution requests (when psychoeducational testing shows that your disability prevents mastery).
  - Accommodation requests sent to instructors.
- Obtain an assessment of your basic skill levels; register

for developmental English or math classes, if needed.
- Enroll in a "Techniques of Study" class.
- Do not overload yourself. Taking twelve credits per term or semester will probably be adequately challenging.
- Schedule your classes so that you have reasonably lengthy breaks between them, and so that they vary in subject matter and intensity.
- Schedule your classes with your "prime time" in mind (e.g., avoid eight a.m. classes if you are a "night owl").

As the Semester Progresses

Not all students with ADD find the same accommodations helpful, and some are successful in college without any special accommodations. However, it is very likely that you could improve your academic record by utilizing some accommodations for your disability. If possible, requests for such accommodations should go to the instructors from the student services office which works with students with disabilities.

In addition, you may also want to talk with your instructors early in the semester, preferably the first week or two of classes, to discuss your needs. This shows that you are concerned about doing well in the class and that you are taking responsibility for your own progress. Find out the instructor's office hours and make an appointment to speak to him/her. In some cases, you may be able to help educate your instructor about ADD. You could offer her/him a copy of Appendix C in this book, or even offer to lend the entire book. Be aware, however, that some instructors may be reluctant to make accommodations in class without official authorization to do so.

At the beginning of the semester, you might:
- Request an appointment with each of your instructors to discuss your accommodation needs.
  - Be prepared to discuss ADD in general, if necessary.

- Take a copy of this book or other written materials to share, as may be appropriate.
- Request specific accommodations, if that is not being done for you by a college office:
  - Permission for a note taker.
  - Permission to tape record lectures.
  - Extended time on tests and other assignments.
  - Alternative testing conditions.
  - Permission to stand or take a break, if needed, during class.
  - Permission to use a calculator, dictionary, or electronic speller during exams.
  - Permission to use a laptop computer during class or on exams.
  - Opportunities to hand in long, written assignments in stages.

After your meeting with an instructor prepare a brief thank you note to him/her for taking the time to talk with you. Not only will she/he feel appreciated, but it will serve as a reminder of who you are and what you need. You may need future meetings with the instructor to remind him/her of the requested accommodations or to ask for additional assistance as the semester progresses.

Additionally, as the semester progresses, you should:
- Contact the disability services office to follow up on and receive the accommodations they assist with.
- Sit in the front of the classroom to optimize your attention.
- Keep a master calendar of all your events, assignments, due dates, appointments, social and family activities.
- Estimate the amount of preparation time for each of your assignments. Break large assignments into smaller tasks.

Plan times and places to complete each task; put them on your master calendar.
- Make a daily "to do" list. Prioritize the list each day.
- Plan your study time; consider it a serious commitment; stick to it.
- Experiment with various study environments until you recognize which one is best for you, then use it. (Some students need an area absolutely free from distractions; others need "white noise," e.g., quiet, calming music which screens out other distractions.)
- If tutoring which is helpful to you is not available free on campus, invest the money to hire a tutor.
- Organize and/or attend study groups.
- Tape your lectures and then listen to them again while walking, jogging, or commuting.
- Quiz yourself by taping questions, pauses, and then the answers. Listen and respond to these tapes while walking, jogging, or commuting.
- Provide rewards for yourself.

Throughout Your College Experience

As you continue through your college experience, it will be important to evaluate continually what is helpful to you, and to repeat those things that work for you. To maximize and reinforce your helpful experiences, it will be especially important to:
- Remember that ADD is a neurologically based disorder.
- Take your medication as prescribed.
- See your counselor on a regular basis.
- Increase structure and reduce distractions.
- Use a calendar and daily "to do" lists, or a "planner," to schedule and prioritize tasks.

- Continue to educate yourself about ADD strategies and accommodations that might be helpful, as well as legal rights and advocacy techniques.

The strategies suggested on the previous pages are a compilation of techniques used by successful students in general and by those with ADD or learning disabilities. It is important that you experiment with these techniques and utilize what is best for you. If you find that you are not being as successful as you would like to be, it is important that you HONESTLY assess which tools you are not utilizing, and use them. Success in college is possible for students with ADD; you have to figure out how to make it possible for you.

(In this section, the author has drawn not only from her education and experience, but also from the works of others: Nadeau, 1994; Quinn, 1994; Richard, 1995.)

Maintain Hope and Positive Attitudes

Self-advocacy is the foundation upon which a successful college experience is built. However, for many college students it is the most difficult step to take. If you know about ADD and how it affects your personality and learning style, and if you can effectively communicate that to educators, you will immediately put yourself at an advantage. Once you have convinced yourself that you are not "lazy, stupid, or crazy" (a phrase from the title of a popular book about adult ADD; see Kelly and Ramundo listed in the references of this book), you will be able to advocate appropriately for yourself. Additionally, you can take responsibility for improving your emotional reactions to college, enhancing your own learning experiences, and maintaining hope and positive attitudes.

One of the larger reactions of the individuals in this book was the changing of their original plans. All of them changed in one way or another. They either extended their completion time, some dropping out temporarily and returning later, or they dropped out altogether. Another outcome is that most of them found success or satisfaction in their careers. However, most of them were not in fields that require the college program they first pursued. We cannot guess why this is true, but it is gratifying to know that despite the obstacles encountered by people with ADD, career satisfaction and success are attainable for those with this diagnosis. It is even more gratifying to know that most of these individuals feel they could be/ were more successful if/when they went back to college after diagnosis and treatment. Most of them felt that the treatment they received for ADD would/did enhance their college success.

These seven individuals with ADD are all unique persons with different backgrounds and experiences. They had different experiences in college and dealt with them in a variety of ways. There were, however, some common patterns in their stories. Their treatments have included behavior modification, facilitated through psychotherapy/counseling, and medication. *Most of them felt there is a positive correlation between treatment for ADD and academic performance.*

An important implication of this for current college students is attitudinal: maintain hope and a positive attitude. Reflecting on the stories of the interviewees discussed in this book, there is reason for hope even if you have failed in the past. Others have faced obstacles similar to yours and have become successful in spite of them. What you can learn from the experiences of other college students with ADD should help you as you strive for your own unique success.

Chapter 10

Study Skills For
College Students with ADD

College life can place a lot of demands on your time that you may not have been used to before. Structuring your learning environments will help you use your time effectively and enhance your learning experiences. A big part of structuring learning environments involves knowing and utilizing some specific study skills. This chapter will discuss time management strategies, environments for studying, note-taking strategies, and test preparation strategies.

Time Management Strategies

If you find yourself having too much to do and too little time to do it, you may want to try some time management strategies to help you budget your time more effectively. Two things are necessary for most time management programs: (1) a system for short- and long-term planning which will help you budget time in the upcoming days, weeks and the entire semester (e.g., a calendar or appointment book), and (2) a daily "to do list" establishing your priorities for the day.

To start, you will need to make a list of activities that require significant amounts of time. Activities can probably be divided into six time categories:
1. class time
2. study time

3. personal chore time
4. work (as in job) time
5. family time
6. recreational time.

Get an appointment book that shows "a week at a glance" and "a month at a glance." First, mark off all the time during the week when you will be attending class. Next, fill in your work schedule if you have a job. Decide on time each day which you can devote to studying and block those times off. Allot some additional time to personal chores (doing laundry, shopping, balancing checkbook, etc.) and family responsibilities and fill in some time each day for recreation.

If your appointment book does not include a "Semester Planner," it would be useful to make one to insert. The "Semester Planner" is very important because it allows you to see the semester "at a glance." On a single sheet of paper you can record major due dates for papers, tests, quizzes, and projects. Then, you can work backwards to set deadlines for yourself to accomplish smaller tasks which lead to the completion of the larger one. You might wish to photocopy the semester planner on the next page and either reduce or enlarge it to fit into your book. If your appointment book is a loose-leaf binder, you could punch holes and insert the semester planner; otherwise you might glue it to the inside book cover.

Write down important dates in your appointment book so you won't miss anything. Include dates when assignments are due, appointments are to be kept, and social and family activities are to be remembered. Get into the habit of carrying your appointment book with you (as you do your other books) and write things down frequently. The more you use your book, the more you will come to rely on it. Check the entries in your appointment book each morning before you start your day, at

Semester Planner

Week	Sunday	Monday	Tuesday	Wednesday	Thursday	Friday	Saturday
1							
2							
3							
4							
5							
6							
7							
8							
9							
10							
11							
12							
13							
14							
15							

least once during the day, and again each night before the day's end.

Use "to do lists" to set your goals and priorities for each day. The "to do list" reminds you of what you need to accomplish for that day. Your list should be prioritized, with the most important objectives underlined or indicated in some way. Those are the ones you really will set your sights on and get completed. Your "to do list" might look like this:

1. *Study for the chemistry test.*
2. *Go to the library to select a book for English.*
3. *Pick up a box of computer disks at the bookstore.*
4. *Buy some socks.*
5. *Be at the dentist's office at 4:30.*

Anything not done by the end of the day will go on the next day's list if it still needs to get done.

Break large tasks down into smaller ones so they don't seem so overwhelming. Set a deadline to accomplish each of the smaller tasks. In no time you will have completed the entire project.

Environment for Studying

Make a commitment to study regularly and stick to it. Set up routines for studying which take into consideration when to study, where to study, and whom to study with.

You may want to experiment with various study times and environments until you recognize which ones are best for you; then use the best time to "hit the books." Some students are "morning people" and prefer to study early in the day. Some are "night people" and find that they study best in the evenings. Get in the habit of following a study routine at the times best suited to your "prime time."

Some students concentrate best in an area absolutely free from distractions; others need "white noise" (e.g., quiet, calming music which screens out other distractions). Others like more activity around them, or find they study best with the radio or TV on. People with ADD report that quiet does not necessarily mean good when it comes to studying. Some like a busy atmosphere and some don't. It is important, however, that you find a place to study that feels right to you.

Figure out whether you study better alone or with a study group. For some subjects you may be better going it alone, whereas for other subjects a study group might really help. Group studying can be especially good when there is a lot of difficult work to wade through and you may not have figured everything out. Study partners can sometimes make studying more interesting and they can rely on one another to answer questions and explain material.

Note-Taking Strategies in Class

It simply is not possible to remember everything an instructor says during a class period. Although an attentive listener may be able to recall main ideas of a lecture for a few days, most details are forgotten fairly quickly, if not immediately. Our memories are only able to retain a limited amount of information.

Accurate note taking ensures that you have a permanent record of information presented in class; it may also enhance alertness, memory, and learning. Note taking can actually help you stay alert in class. By keeping busy (with note taking) your mind is actively engaged and you are less likely to daydream. So, even if you don't need notes in a class, taking some can actually help you pay attention better. In addition, because you activate different senses and modalities (kinesthetic, motor, internal speech) when you take notes, you may also stimulate memory functions and recall information better.

Taking good notes in class is a skill which students usually acquire by trial and error rather than being taught. Most people develop their own personal style of note taking that works best for them. However, there are some strategies in note taking that might work well for everyone:

1. It is important that your notes are well organized. Notes for a particular subject should be kept in one section of a notebook with pages numbered and dated. Some people use a looseleaf notebook with course dividers for this purpose. Others prefer individual spiral notebooks for each course.

2. When taking notes it is helpful to distinguish important from unimportant information so you can avoid writing down everything the instructor says. Often, an instructor will give you clues (raises voice, repeats information, gives one or more examples to illustrate and emphasize a point, tells you something will be on an exam) to what information she/he feels is important. The detail you use in your note taking will depend partly on the emphasis the instructor puts on the sources of information available to you, e.g., lecture notes, assigned reading from a text, supplementary reading.

3. Notes should be organized by main topics and supporting ideas, or at the very least headings should be used to identify the beginning of a new topic or section. Some people prefer to take notes in outline form. The following outline illustrates such an approach:

I. Main topic
  A. Supporting idea
  B. Supporting idea
      1. sub-idea or example
      2. sub-idea or example
II. Main topic
  A. Supporting idea
      1. sub-idea or example
      2. sub-idea or example
  B. Supporting idea
  C. Supporting idea

Some people write down verbatim statements or summaries of what the instructor says. It is not necessary to write verbatim statements unless the instructor directs you to do so. Summarizing, using at least some of your own words, increases understanding. Outlining, verbatim statements and/or summaries can be combined.

4.   Study skills specialists at Cornell University suggest a method of note taking which is especially effective for test preparation (Holkeboer, 1996). They suggest that you divide a notebook page so that you have a fold or line 2 1/2 inches from the left side (see page 132). Then take notes on the right 6 inches of the page, writing only on one side of the paper. When class is over, review notes taken on the right 6 inches of the page to pick out the main topics from that information. Record these main topics, using a few words for each, in the left 2 1/2 inch column. When it is time to study for a test, fold the paper so the class notes are

Effective Note-taking and Listening Skills in Class

Notes help:	A. Why take notes?
organize	1. helps you organize what you hear.
exams	2. helps when you study for exams.
concentrate	3. helps maintain attention.
information	4. the information may not be available elsewhere.

B. How do you take notes?

How?
  prepare

1. be prepared:
   a. study and read prior to class
   b. have a purpose for listening
   c. attitude--you are not there to be entertained but to learn.

develop system

2. have a system--be organized:
   a. outline, dash, number or sentence form
   b. use a note column and a recall column
   c. use symbols--make sure you will know what they mean later.

near front

3. sit near the front of the class, keep eyes on professor:
   a. helps you concentrate
   b. eliminates some visual distractions.

listen then write

4. listen before writing:
   a. listen, understand, evaluate, organize, then write--listen long enough to be sure to undertand--then write
   b. listen for signal words--"first," "most important," "finally"
   c. leave spaces if you miss something--fill it in later
   d. lead, don't follow--anticipate where the prof is taking you
   e. be selective, brief and concise--omit anecdotes, long examples
   f. associate your past experiences and knowledge with what the prof is saying.

C. What to do if you have problems:

If problem:
  tell prof

1. tell the prof if:
   a. s/he is going too fast, or not loud enough
   b. his/her purpose or main idea is not clear
   c. you are not sure about the relationship of ideas--may ask to draw a diagram, illustrate with an example.

miss something

2. if you miss something important:
   a. ask the prof after class
   b. check with another student.

need additional help

3. if you need more information or help about the subject:
   a. ask the prof if old exams are available
   b. talk with students who have had the course--ask for old notes, handouts, exams.

(Lietz, 1987)

folded under. You can then use the main topics to quiz yourself on the information. The previous notes on a lecture about "Effective Note-Taking and Listening Skills in Class" illustrate the Cornell system of note taking.

5. To save time, notes often contain abbreviations and symbols for commonly used words or phrases. Sample abbreviations and symbols are:

re:	regarding, about	def	definition
etc.	et cetera	#	number
+	and	%	percent
-	no, not	4	for
=	equal	b4	before
w/	with	b/c	because
w/o	without	e.g.	example
@	each, at	wd	word
assoc	association	p.	page
co.	company	exc.	except
info	information	...	repeats pattern
amt	amount	$	money
cont.	continued	>	greater than
cf.	compare	<	less than
n.b.	important	?	question

6. Any new vocabulary or terminology that is unfamiliar to you should be underlined and defined to increase your understanding of the subject.

7. Review notes as soon after class as possible, filling in any gaps. Forgetting takes place almost immediately, and a review when the material is fresh in your mind enhances your chances of remembering it.

8. Before each class, review the notes taken in that class previously and do all newly assigned reading so you can get the most out of the class period.

9. If you are unable to focus attention in class enough to take notes or if you are unable keep up with the instructor when taking notes, ask permission to tape record lectures so you can listen to them again. Try not to do this too much, though, because it takes time to attend class and to listen to the tape all over again.

10. Taking notes from books is also quite important, as it will save you time when you need to review or study for an exam or prepare to write a paper. Note cards may be used to write down important information. Write the source of each note on the top of the card and write a brief summary of the information read. Label the card by topic and put all cards with the same topic together.

Test Preparation Strategies

Preparation for an examination starts at the beginning of the semester when you receive the course syllabus or outline. This tells you what the instructor intends to cover and the sources of information that will be used throughout the course. Begin by making sure you have all the books necessary to study from.

Review Information Frequently

One of the unfortunate characteristics of the human mind is that our memory tends to decay over time so material that has to be remembered well needs to be studied and restudied if it is to be retained in memory. Memory traces become stronger with each repetition. Repetition is the only way information is stored in long-term memory. Therefore, it makes sense that the more you review material in a course, the more easily you will remember information at examination time.

It also makes sense that our minds are better at remembering information that we understand than remembering information that is learned by rote. Generally, you do not forget as quickly information which has been understood and organized in your mind by certain principles. Thus, it is important to review notes and passages, think about their meaning, and try to integrate the information in some meaningful way rather than to just memorize it.

Use the SQ4R Method

A popular method for studying is the SQ4R method. SQ4R stands for Survey, Question, Read, "Rite" (write), Recite, Review.

- Survey the sections to be studied in your text by looking over the main headings and the subheadings in those sections.
- Make up questions about the information surveyed.
- Read the sections entirely.
- "Rite" (write) the answers to the questions.
- Recite the information, out loud if possible.
- Review your work.

During the survey step of the SQ4R method you should skim through the sections to be studied in order to get an overview of the material. Next, take each portion of your reading and, from the heading or subheading, formulate one or two questions about the material. Then read those sections entirely and write the answers to the questions you made up. Recite the answers to your questions out loud along with other important points to be remembered in each section of your reading. After going through an entire section, frequently review the information you covered and write down key words or phrases in margins or on note cards, or highlight with a marker.

Use Movement, Stimulation and Conversation to Stay Alert While Studying

Based on the premise that an active mind will stay more alert than a passive mind, you should try to make the process of studying as active as possible. Instead of just reading to study, combine reading with underlining, writing in margins in your book, highlighting with colored markers, and reciting important information out loud. All these activities can help your mind stay active and alert during the study process. These strategies may be especially important for people with ADD, since they have a tendency to be less alert than others and may benefit from stimulation during the tedious process of studying.

Don't try to study for too long without a break. Frequent breaks from studying can be more beneficial than marathon study sessions. If you eat during study breaks, avoid caffeine and sugar. Study with a group or a "study buddy" if you find that you have trouble concentrating when you are alone. Another person can sometimes keep you on track and focused. Studying with others adds diversity to the activity.

Structuring your learning environment will improve your chances for success in college. Utilizing specific study strategies is one way of structuring your environment. Experiment until you find your best time management strategies, study environments, note-taking techniques and test preparation strategies. **Success in college is possible!**

Chapter 11

Implications for Educators and Counselors

The doors of higher education are opening wider for many groups of people with disabilities in our society. Postsecondary education and future employability are becoming increasingly intertwined ("Education," 1990). If we want the best possible workforce for a healthy national economy, we want the best possible education for all of our citizens.

This book, which provides information about the college experiences of adults with ADD, has implications for educators and counselors who work with college students with ADD. Hopefully, the experiences of the people portrayed here will provide a basis to better understand the difficulties that having ADD poses for students in higher education. Colleges and universities need to be aware of these issues in order to provide equal opportunities for higher education for this group of students.

Federal legislation which protects the needs of citizens with disabilities applies to colleges and universities that have students with ADD. ADD, when it is of sufficient severity, has been legally established as a disability which affords certain mandated rights. Section 504 of the Rehabilitation Act (RA) of 1973 is a civil rights law prohibiting discrimination against persons with disabilities. All educational institutions that receive federal funds must comply with Section 504 by addressing the needs of students with disabilities as adequately as the

needs of nondisabled individuals (CHADD, 1993a). Furthermore, the Americans with Disabilities Act (ADA), enacted in
1990, requires all educational institutions to meet the needs of
those with disabilities (including ADD). (Specific applicable
citations from regulations for these laws appear in Chapter 9.)

Legal requirements aside, accommodating students with
ADD is important because it relates to the mission of colleges
and universities. Addressing the broad issue of ADA compli-
ance, Shepherd et al. (1992) identified this link between accommodation and mission. They stated:

> ADA compliance—making access to education a priority—is
> consistent with the mission and purpose of community colleges
> and four-year colleges and universities .... Community colleges
> have long recognized their obligations to their local communities
> to make higher education accessible to persons from all walks of
> life, and their mission statements reflect these beliefs. Many four-
> year colleges and universities have modified their mission
> statements along similar lines .... Institutions dedicated to
> improving "access" to higher education should place the same
> emphasis on physical barriers, communication barriers, attitudi-
> nal barriers towards persons with disabilities as they do other
> types of barriers, such as economic barriers. (p.3)

It certainly is within the mission of higher education to provide understanding and accessible education to students with
ADD.

What Can Counselors and Educators Do?

For many counselors and educators, new awareness about
learners with ADD can produce new attitudes that can support
the educational purpose of our institutions. We can support
ADD advocacy, so that erroneously adverse preconceptions

of students' abilities do not jeopardize their educational and occupational opportunities. Educators can be alert for ways to bolster the self-esteem of students with ADD. We can also be alert for ways to motivate these students and reinforce their efforts to learn (e.g., by communicating a caring attitude, treating the students with respect, avoiding intimidation, and being approachable). Methods that might motivate students with ADD and enhance their self-esteem are probably those that are effective for students in general, but ADD students might have a special need for them.

Interventions to Use with Students with ADD

"What it takes is for someone to get up in front of class and have a little bit of stimuli to them, then we're 'suck city': anything that comes out of their mouth gets pulled right in .... He (referring to a professor) had tons of fire. That man was a walking firecracker waiting for him to explode all the time. I learned a lot. He was good. We never had an empty seat in that class. Everybody came to that class."— Keith

Unfortunately, there is no research to direct us on what educational interventions are most effective for college students with ADD. Most of what we think will be effective is inferred from the research done with students in elementary and secondary education and from what students and instructors in higher education tell us works. Effective interventions usually focus on several variables:
- modification of educators' attitudes and behavior
- modification of the learning environment
- accommodations and support services.

Attitudes and Belief Systems

The *CHADD Educators Manual* (Fowler, 1992) is the most comprehensive handbook about ADD and education that is available. It was written by Mary Fowler in collaboration with Russell Barkley, Ph.D., Ron Reeve, Ph.D., and Sydney Zentall, Ph.D. Fowler's collaborators have all conducted substantial scholarly research on the topic of ADD. The authors discussed the important impact that parents and educators can have on the lives of individuals with ADD. Although this work was written with elementary and secondary school students in mind, many of the points the authors make can apply to postsecondary education as well. They stated:

> If we, the parents and educators of such children, are to have any effect at all in changing the negative outcomes that result from this disability, we have to take the first step. That step is CHANGE OUR BELIEF SYSTEM. We must ACCEPT that ADD is a disability, and that these children behave in a way that comes naturally to them. (p. 8)

They quoted Dr. Ross Greene, Assistant Professor of Psychiatry and Pediatrics at the University of Massachusetts Medical Center, who said:

> First you have to establish the level of understanding and knowledge on the part of everybody concerned. To the extent that knowledge, attitudes, and beliefs guide a person's behavior, these factors may have considerable impact upon a teacher's interactions with the student with ADD. (p. 8)

The foundation of sound interventions by educators, then, is an expanded knowledge base, increased understanding, and acceptance of ADD for what it is.

Fowler (1992) stated, "Psychology has long embraced the notion that people, environments, and individuals are either suited to each other (good matches), or they are not (poor matches)." She related that anecdotal reports have told us that school success for children with ADD varies from year to year and that the teacher is the most commonly cited reason for the experience having been positive or negative.

Fowler cited Greene, who provided a list of 20 teacher characteristics that are likely indicators of positive student outcomes, characteristics he had gleaned from the work of researchers on disabilities. He listed the following:

1. Positive academic expectations.
2. Frequent monitoring and checking student work.
3. Clarity (e.g., clear directions, standards, expectations).
4. Flexibility (adapts as necessary, e.g., to modifications needed by certain students, schedule changes).
5. Fairness (lack of favoritism).
6. Active involvement with students (remains actively involved with students as they work).
7. Responsiveness (attention to students' responses and comments).
8. Warmth (good relationship with students, receptive to students' approaches).
9. Patience.
10. Humor.
11. Structure (highly structured, predictable lessons).
12. Consistency (sets and maintains contingencies).
13. Firmness.
14. Knowledge of different types of behavioral interventions.

15. Positive attitude toward mainstreaming.
16 Knowledge and/or willingness to learn about work-
    ing with students with emotional and behavioral prob-
    lems and exceptional children in general.
17. Willingness to work with special education teacher
    (e.g., share information regarding student's progress,
    seek assistance when needed, participate in meetings
    or conferences involving students).
18. High perception of self-efficacy (perceives self as
    competent teacher).
19. High sense of involvement (professional responsibil-
    ity).
20. High professional job satisfaction. (pp. 34-35)

Learning Environment
Zametkin (1991) elaborated on the type of environment in
which people with ADD perform best: high structure, low
distractibility, consistent positive reinforcement, consistent
limit-setting, consistent consequences for inappropriate behavior, highly nurturing. CHADD (Children and Adults With Attention Deficit Disorders), a national support organization, published a document called *CHADD Facts 5, Attention Deficit
Disorders: An Educator's Guide* (1993b). They, too, stated
that the effective classroom environment for the student with
ADD is generally highly ordered and predictable. They listed
three general categories in which educators can modify the
classroom environment: classroom organization, classroom
management and curriculum.

*"Any time there were classes that, for instance on the black-
board there were illustrations, that would keep my attention*

*.... Also, if I were distracted, I could come back and I had
something there to put me right back on track. Where a
lecture, if you've lost two or three minutes of his lecture,
then try to focus, you've missed it because there is nothing
there to bring you up to speed."— Mike*

Martin et al. (1984) indicated that academic tasks and
teacher expectations need to take into account the student's
short attention span. They suggested that assignments should
be brief initially, then extended gradually as the student's ca-
pabilities increase. They also endorsed the environment described by Zametkin (1991): freedom from extraneous stimuli,
behavior modification, and token reinforcement for modify-
ing inappropriate behaviors and improving academic performance. Barkley (1990) suggested adapting some behavior
modification methods and self-control therapies for the young
adult with ADD trying to meet the demands of a college or
vocational training program.

Accommodations and Supportive Services
Specific accommodations and supportive services for college
students with ADD are suggested by the themes that emerge in
the interviews which were summarized in Chapters 4, 5, and
6. Inattention and/or hyperactivity-impulsivity are essential
characteristics of the disorder and should always be taken into
account by educators when they are more frequent and severe
than is developmentally appropriate. We must also consider
how the features of this disorder affect the specific individual
with whom we are dealing. In the providing of appropriate
interventions and accommodations, there are roles for college
administrations, for teaching faculty, and for counselors.

College Administrators

<u>Policy Formation</u>
When formulating policy that might impact students with ADD, administrators should consider providing:
- Admission decisions with special considerations.
- Assessments of basic skills.
- Priority registration.
- Provisions for single dormitory rooms.
- Priority hiring—consideration to staff who are sensitive to accommodating students.
- Reconsideration for those who receive diagnosis after academic dismissal.
- Substitute course requirements (e.g., instead of math and foreign language) when psycho-educational testing shows that the disability prevents mastery.

<u>Program Development</u>
When developing programs for students with ADD, administrators should consider providing:
- An office of disability services, staffed by qualified professionals.
- Special orientation programs for students with ADD and/or learning disabilities.
- Developmental courses, especially in English and math.
- Alternative environments for studying and learning.
- Study skills classes.
- Supportive individual and/or group counseling provided by a qualified professional counselor.
- Staff to act as note takers, tutors, and editors for students.

- Recorded textbooks, such as Recordings for the Blind.
- ADD support groups.

Staff Supervision
When supervising staff, administrators should consider providing:
- In-service training opportunities.
- Support for attending conferences related to ADD.
- Membership in Children and Adults with Attention Deficit Disorders (CHADD) and/or Association on Higher Education and Disabilities (AHEAD).

(See also Appendix B, ADMIN.)

Teaching Faculty

Attitudes and Affect
Through attitudes and affective behaviors, teaching faculty can do the following to provide positive environment and heightened self-esteem for students with ADD:
- Demonstrate knowledge of the possible effects of ADD on academic achievement, and reflect empathy.
- Reinforce positive behavior with compliments.
- Provide reassurance and encouragement.
- Look for opportunities for students to display leadership or expertise.
- Make time to talk with a student alone.

Teaching Strategies
In the classroom, teaching faculty can employ the following strategies to assist students with ADD:
- Provide students with a detailed course syllabus.

- Provide in clear, concise, written communication the course expectations, due dates, and grading.
- Begin lectures with a concise review of what was covered previously and an outline (ideally, written) of what will follow.
- Provide classroom stimuli by being dynamic, animated, expressive (e.g., by telling stories, moving around the room, and interacting with students).
- Vary instructional methods.
- Reinforce basic skills by incorporating reading and writing across the curriculum.
- Provide visual and hands-on learning opportunities when needed and reasonably possible.
- Present new or technical vocabulary on an overhead, on the chalkboard, or in a handout.
- Call on students only when their hands are raised if there are impulsive, overly talkative students in the class.
- Give clear, concise instructions.
- Provide assignments both orally and in writing.
- Break long assignments into smaller parts, providing feedback between the parts when possible.
- Permit students to tape record lectures.
- Encourage students to stand or take a break during class.
- Remind students to check their work, especially if performance appears rushed or sloppy.
- Permit the use of calculators, dictionaries, and electronic spellers during exams.
- Provide prompt feedback about performance.

Class Management
In their class management policies and procedures, instruc-

tors can be accommodating to students with ADD by:
- Making the syllabus available before registration.
- Allowing partial credit, if not full, for late assignments.
- Encouraging promptness, but not penalizing grades for tardiness.

Encouraging the Use of Accommodations
Teaching faculty can encourage students to utilize accommodations by referring them to the office of disabilities services, or by utilizing the following:
- Reasonable academic modifications after receiving documentation of disability.
- Accommodations that do not offer an advantage, but provide equal opportunity:
  - Alternative test-taking arrangements.
  - Extended deadlines.
  - Note takers.
  - Tape recorders.
  - Laptop computers.
  - Exams with extra time, over a period of time, or in short segments.
  - Alternative physical environments for test taking.
  - Opportunities to hand in long, written assignments in stages.

(See also Appendix C, TEACH.)

Counselors

Attitudes and Affect
Through attitudes and affective behaviors, counselors can do
the following to provide a positive environment and height-
ened self-esteem for students with ADD:
- Remember— it is a neurological disorder.
- Demonstrate knowledge of the possible effects of ADD
  on academic achievement, and reflect empathy.
- Reinforce positive behavior with compliments.
- Provide reassurance and encouragement.
- Speak softly and non-threateningly.
- Convey that many adults with ADD are successful
  people.

Goals
Counselors can formulate treatment plans for students with
ADD appropriate to their diagnoses and the manifestations of
their disabilities. Treatment goals for the counselor might in-
clude the following:
- Assist with education about the disorder.
- Help in the understanding of the ramifications of the
  disorder in all aspects of life.
- Assist with long-term goal formulation, including ca-
  reer planning.
- Assist with short-term goal setting.
- Utilize cognitive remediation strategies or "coaching"
  to enhance attention.
- Provide treatment for coexisting conditions (e.g., de-
  pression, anxiety, substance abuse).
- Identify unique strengths and weaknesses.
- Formulate an academic plan which limits course load

and spreads out the time and intensity of classes.
- Recommend instructors who have reputations for accommodating students with disabilities.
- Maintain focus on dealing with one issue at a time, while remaining cognizant of the entire picture.
- Interpret psychological motivations for behavior cautiously (e.g., lateness might stem from disorganization rather than resistance to therapy).
- Read and analyze course syllabi with students so expectations are understood and time management is facilitated.
- Model the use of calendars to plan personal, academic, and social activities.
- Teach study skills techniques (e.g., time management, use of notebooks with dividers, memory techniques).
- Teach relaxation techniques.
- Employ behavior management techniques to modify troublesome behaviors (e.g., to control anger, to manage stress).
- Process appropriate social skills and problem-solving techniques.
- Promote the building of self-esteem by empowering the student.
- Provide counseling to the family, if necessary.

Support Techniques
Counselors can provide students with ADD with supportive counseling by:
- Looking for signs of stress build-up and encouraging students to use stress-reducing techniques.
- Encouraging students to advocate for themselves.
- Reminding them to use medication as prescribed (they

sometimes are in denial or forget the effects).
- Promoting ADD support groups and/or other self-help groups.
- Encouraging physical exercise and spiritual development.

Referral

Counselors might provide referrals to students with ADD for:
- Medication management, to a physician knowledgeable about ADD.
- Identification of their disability, to the appropriate institutional authorities (e.g., Office of Disability Services), in order to obtain accommodations.
- Diagnostic testing to assess learning disabilities.
- Assessment testing for better self-understanding, for goal-setting and career planning.

(In this section on interventions and accommodations, the author has drawn not only from her education and experience but also from the work of others: Nadeau, 1994; Parker, 1992; Quinn, 1994; Richard, 1995; Weinstein, 1994.)

Summary

Counselors and educators need to understand and accommodate students with ADD for many reasons. Through understanding ADD and knowing what assistance is appropriate and possible, as educators, we not only can advocate among ourselves for these students, but also can provide interventions and accommodations. Some of these techniques are strategies that may be helpful to students in general. However, ADD is not manifested in all individuals in the same way. Thus, other accommodations and interventions will be specific to an individual's disability. See Appendices B, C and D for a summary of interventions for educators and counselors.

Although obtaining a college education is not easy for most students with ADD, there is evidence that success is possible, and that the process can be made easier through the collaboration of students, counselors and educators. Students have a heavy responsibility for self-advocacy and for structuring their learning environment, utilizing interventions and accommodations. However, success depends both on the individual with the disorder and on the efforts of educators. My hope is that this book has provided a greater understanding of individuals with ADD. I hope students will read the book themselves and will give it to their counselors and educators, and that it will contribute to collaboration for students' success.

Appendix A
Students'
TIPS
(Time management, Interventions,
Positive attitudes, Supports)
for Getting the Most Out of College

Time management

- Arrange to live in a single dorm room or apartment
- Do not overload yourself --12 credits per term is probably enough
- Schedule classes with reasonably lengthy breaks between them
- Schedule classes so they vary in subject matter and intensity
- Keep your "prime time" in mind when scheduling
- Maintain a calendar of all events--assignments, appointments, social
- Break large assignments into smaller tasks to put on your calendar
- Make and prioritize a "to do" list daily
- Plan study time and consider it a serious commitment

Interventions

- Select a college that has services and support you need
- Have a complete treatment plan in place: MEDICATION, COUNSELING and EDUCATION
- Establish realistic goals
- Attend to physical well-being —exercise, nutrition, sleep
- Develop your spiritual well-being
- Know about your limitations and needed accommodations
- Obtain career counseling from someone familiar with your disabilities
- Share records of your disabilities with those providing assistance
- Request assistance —priority registration, course substitutions, taped textbooks, proctored tests, tutoring, note takers
- Register for developmental English and/or math classes, if needed
- Enroll in a study skills class

- Sit in the front of the room
- Experiment with various study environments until you recognize your best
- Invest in tutoring if it is not available free
- Organize and/or attend study groups
- Tape lectures and listen to them again while walking, jogging, or commuting
- Quiz yourself by taping questions, pauses, and answers; listen and respond to tapes while walking, jogging, or commuting
- Take medication as prescribed
- See counselor or therapist on a regular basis
- Increase structure and reduce distractions
- Educate yourself about ADD—strategies, legal rights, and advocacy

P ositive attitudes

- Advocate appropriately
- Participate in extracurricular activities you enjoy
- Celebrate small successes
- Remember that ADD is a neurologically based disorder
- Listen to or read the success stories of other students with ADD

S upports

- Seek accommodating instructors
- Develop a supportive relationship with a counselor or therapist
- Talk about problems with appropriate persons
- Participate in an ADD support group or start one
- Request an appointment with each instructor—discuss your needs, explain ADD if necessary
- Request accommodations—note taker, permission to tape, extended time, alternative testing conditions, permission to stand or take breaks, calculators or electronic spellers during exams, permission to hand in long assignments in stages

Appendix B
College Administrators
ADMIN
(Advocacy, Decisions, Memberships, Instruction, Necessities)
for Students with ADD

A dvocacy
- Provide special orientation for those with ADD and/or LD
- Support individual/group counseling by qualified counselors
- Initiate ADD support groups
- Provide in-service training opportunities for staff
- Provide support for staff participation in conferences on ADD

D ecisions
- Consider readmission for those diagnosed after academic dismissal
- Make admissions decisions with special considerations
- Provide priority registration
- Allow provisions for single dormitory rooms
- Substitute course requirements when psycho-educational testing shows that the disability prevents mastery

M emberships
- Support staff or institutional membership in Children and Adults with Attention Deficit Disorder (CHADD) and /or the Association on Higher Education and Disability (AHEAD)

I nstruction
- Priority hiring to faculty sensitive to accommodating students
- Have office of disability services, staffed by those who know ADD
- Provide developmental courses—especially English and math
- Develop study skills classes
- Hire staff to act as note takers, tutors, and editors for students
- Provide for recorded textbooks

N ecessities
- Comply with State and Federal regulations
- Assess basic skills
- Provide alternative environments for studying and learning

Appendix C
College Teaching Faculty
TEACH
(Techniques, Encouragement, Accommodations,
Classroom policies, Help)
for Students with ADD

T echniques

- Provide clear, concise, written course expectations
- Begin lectures with review and outline
- Provide stimuli by being dynamic, animated
- Vary instructional methods
- Incorporate basic skills (e.g., reading, writing)
- Provide visual and hands-on experiences
- Use overhead, chalkboard, or handout for new vocabulary
- Call only on students whose hands are raised
- Give clear, concise instructions
- Provide assignments orally and in writing
- Break long assignments into smaller parts
- Provide feedback frequently
- Permit tape recorders during lectures
- Encourage breaks or standing
- Remind students to check work

E ncouragement

- Acknowledge effects of ADD on academics
- Provide positive reinforcement
- Reassure and encourage
- Look for opportunities for displays of leadership or expertise

A ccommodations

- Utilize reasonable modifications upon documentation
- Offer accommodations that provide equal opportunities
- Provide alternative test-taking arrangements
- Extend deadlines

- Obtain note takers
- Encourage the use of tape recorders
- Suggest utilization of laptop computers
- Test with extra time, over a period of time, or in short segments
- Find alternative physical environments for test-taking
- Allow long assignments to be completed in stages

Classroom management

- Make syllabus available before registration
- Accept reports in non-written forms
- Allow partial credit, if not full, for late assignments
- Encourage promptness, but do not penalize grades for tardiness

Help

- Refer for counseling
- Refer to tutors
- Give assistance during office hours
- Make time to talk with student alone

Appendix D
Counselors
TARGETS
(Testing, Attitudes, Referrals, Goal Setting, Education, Techniques, Support)
for Use with Students with ADD

T esting

- Test to assess for learning disabilities
- Assess for better self-understanding, goal setting, and career planning

A ttitudes

- Remember —it is a neurological disorder
- Demonstrate knowledge of the possible effects of ADD on academic achievement

R eferrals

- Recommend instructors with reputations for accommodating students with disabilities
- Refer to physicians knowledgeable about medication management for ADD
- Identify disability to the appropriate institutional authorities to obtain accommodations
- Refer to other mental health professionals, if necessary

G oal Setting

- Assist with long-term goal formulation, including career planning
- Assist with short-term goal setting
- Formulate an academic plan which limits course load and spreads out the time and intensity of classes
- Read and analyze course syllabi with students so expectations are understood and time management is facilitated

- Promote the building of healthy self-esteem by empowering the student.

E ducation

- Assist with education about the disorder
- Promote understanding of the impact of the disorder on all aspects of life
- Provide counseling to the family, if necessary

T echniques

- Speak softly and non-threateningly
- Reinforce positive behavior with compliments
- Utilize cognitive behavioral strategies or "coaching" to enhance attention
- Provide treatment for coexisting conditions
- Identify unique strengths and weaknesses
- Maintain focus on dealing with one issue at a time
- Interpret psychological motivations for behavior cautiously
- Model the use of calendars to plan personal, academic, and social activities
- Teach relaxation techniques
- Employ behavior management techniques to modify troublesome behavior
- Process appropriate social skills and problem-solving techniques
- Look for signs of stress build-up and teach students stress-reducing techniques

S upport

- Provide reassurance and encouragement
- Encourage students to advocate for themselves
- Remind them to use treatment as prescribed

Appendix E

Research Methods and Interview Questions

In this study, I used interviews to gather descriptions of the college experiences of seven adults with ADD who had been diagnosed by the same psychiatrist. Gorden (1980) stated, "There is much literature devoted to studies and experiments on the relative value of interview. Interviewing is most valuable when we are interested in knowing people's beliefs, attitudes, values, knowledge, or any other subjective orientations or mental content" (p. 11). Bogdan and Biklen (1982) pointed out that interviews are used to gather descriptive data in the interviewees' own words so that the researcher can develop insights into how the interviewees interpret some piece of the world. In this study interviews helped me discover the interviewees' knowledge and subjective orientations. The data collected in the interviews helped me develop insights into how these individuals interpreted their college experiences.

Research Design

Research Questions
The main research question was: How do students with Attention Deficit Disorder (ADD) experience this disorder in their college life and deal with the experiences this disorder presents? The answer to this question draws on the answers to

subsidiary questions.

Some research questions evoked background information. That information provided a basis for understanding answers to subsequent research questions. The background information questions were as follows.

1. Demographics
   a. What is the individual's age?
   b. What is the individual's gender?
   c. What is the individual's race?
   d. When did he/she attend college?
   e. Where did he/she attend college?
   f. For how long did he/she attend college?
   g. Which of the 14 DSM III-R characteristics have been exhibited by the individual?
   h. What is the individual's current educational or occupational status?
2. Understanding of Attention Deficit Disorder
   a. What is the individual's understanding of ADD?
   b. Where did he/she obtain most of his/her knowledge about the disorder?
3. Feelings About ADD
   a. How does the individual feel about having ADD?
   b. How does the individual feel about being labeled ADD?
   c. Has the individual ever felt that he/she was different from others because he/she had ADD?
4. Personal History
   a. What was the individual's experience in being diagnosed with ADD?
   b. Has he/she ever been diagnosed as having any learning disabilities?
   c. What history does he/she have with medication?
   d. What does he/she remember about experiences in elementary or high school that might be related to ADD?
   e. Was he/she ever retained in a grade? If so, what kind of messages did that give to him/her?
   f. How does the individual characterize his/her relationships with friends and family?
      (1) What were the reactions of others to problems related to ADD?
      (2) Did he/she tell friends/co-workers about the ADD?

(3) Has he/she experienced any difficulties in his/her dating/ marriage relationships that he/she attributes to ADD?

Some research questions elicited data about the interviewees' experiences in college. These questions were as follows:

5.   Selection of College and Admission
    a.   How did the individual select the college attended?
    b.   What, if any, problems did he/she encounter in being admitted to college?

6.   College Teaching/Learning Preferences
    a.   What kinds of classes did he/she prefer (lecture, discussion, etc.; self-paced, regular classroom, laboratory, etc.; small, large)?
    b.   What types of instructional delivery did he/she prefer (auditory, visual, etc.)?

Other research questions elicited data about how the interviewees dealt with their experiences. These questions were as follows:

7.   Study Techniques and Support Mechanisms While in College
    a.   What types of study habits/study environments did he/she have?
    b.   What types of coping mechanisms did he/she employ?
    c.   What special services did he/she obtain from the college?
    d.   Were there any special accommodations available at the college to assist in studying, test-taking, etc.?
    e.   Did he/she attempt to receive any special help (tutoring, special instruction) from anyone, either within the college or outside of the college?

8.   General Problems in College
    a.   What, if any, problems were encountered while in college?
    b.   Did he/she feel a need to struggle to concentrate/focus in classes or while studying?
    c.   Did his/her performance ever vary greatly from one time to another?

9.   Relationships with Instructors
    a.   Did the personality/attitude of the instructor make a difference in his/her learning?
    b.   What were the instructors' reactions to problems?
    c.   Did the individual tell instructors about ADD?

10.   Advice
    a.   What advice does the individual have for college instructors who have students with ADD in their classrooms?

b.   What advice does the individual have for students with ADD who are going to college?

Selection Criteria

Before referring her patients to me, the psychiatrist briefly described the purpose of the research to them. She also assured them that she knew me personally, that I am a professional counselor, and that I would handle their reports in a professional and confidential manner. The psychiatrist obtained a release-of-information form from each of the participants. She then provided me with the name, address, phone number, and birth date for each of them. I contacted each participant and obtained a written consent form before I interviewed them.

Anonymity and Confidentiality

Before I began asking questions in my first interview with each participant, I reviewed the policies of confidentiality and anonymity. Additionally, I explained to each participant that pseudonyms would be used to protect their identity. That policy has been carried out in presenting the data in this book. The names of organizations and the individuals, and other identifying information, have been changed to protect the anonymity of those being studied. Care has been taken not to alter substantive information.

Data Collection

Type of Data

Each participant was interviewed at length at least twice. The first interviews lasted between 45 minutes and 1.5 hours. The second interviews lasted between 45 minutes and 2 hours.

Those who had shorter interviews the first time tended to have longer interviews the second time. All interviews were audiotaped. First interviews were transcribed. I listened to the second interviews repeatedly and took notes. In some cases, individuals were telephoned and asked to clarify data for accuracy. Notes were taken about these telephone conversations.

Interviews

A standardized, nonscheduled type of interview was used. "Standardized" (in relation to "nonstandardized") refers to collecting precisely the same categories of information from a number of respondents. "Nonscheduled" interviews (in relation to "scheduled" interviews) are those in which the interviewer need not ask questions in the same order with all interviewees, and is free to use alternative wording.

Data Analysis

The process of data analysis began when I was interviewing the participants and continued through several months of scrutinizing transcriptions and audiotapes. I began to see some patterns emerging even after interviewing the first few individuals the first time. After I interviewed all the participants once, I had the audiotapes transcribed. I studied the transcriptions, making notes on themes, ideas, and areas for further investigation. I then formulated questions for each participant that I wanted to ask him/her in a second interview.

I interviewed each individual a second time and audiotaped the interviews. Afterwards, I listened to the audiotapes and took general notes about the interactions. Then I studied my notes from the transcriptions and my notes from the tapes, again noting themes and topics that emerged. I developed a coding system and searched the data for regularities and patterns. Then I developed assertions and matched the data with the assertions. I selected assertions that dealt most specifically with college experiences, and that had a substantial amount of supporting data. I then reviewed the data for each assertion to be sure that the data supported the assertion. I altered the assertions to convey each idea most accurately before writing my final analysis.

Appendix F

Resources

Organizations

ADDA
Attention Deficit Disorder Association
P.O. Box 972
Mentor, Ohio 44061
(800) 487-2282

ADDA is a national organization which has been active in addressing the needs of adults with attention deficit disorders. Through its annual conference on adult issues, ADDA has succeeded in bringing important information to the forefront.

AHEAD
Association on Higher Education and Disability
P.O. Box 21192
Columbus, Ohio 43221-0192
(614) 488-4972

AHEAD provides information regarding disability issues in higher education on a national level. It offers several publications and provides information on recent rulings by the Office of Civil Rights. Several of the publications are disability specific.

CHADD
Children and Adults with Attention Deficit Disorders
National Headquarters
499 Northwest 70th Avenue, Suite 101
Plantation, Florida 33317
(305) 587-3700 • (800) 233-4050
Internet: http://www.chadd.org

CHADD is the nation's largest organization for children and adults with attention deficit disorders. CHADD's mission is to provide information and support to those affected by ADD. It maintains over 600 chapters throughout the United States. Members receive current information on ADD through excellent publications, which include fact sheets, newsletters, and a news magazine, *Attention!* CHADD sponsors an annual international conference on ADD which attracts parents, educators and health professionals from around the world.

HEATH
Higher Education and the Handicapped
One Dupont Circle, Suite 670
Washington, D.C. 20036-1193
(800) 54-HEATH

The HEATH Resources Center maintains a National Clearinghouse on Postsecondary Education for Handicapped Individuals. The Center provides information about educational support services, policies, procedures, adaptations, and opportunities in colleges, vocational-technical schools, adult education programs, etc.

LDAA
Learning Disability Association of America
4156 Library Road
Pittsburgh, Pennsylvania 15234
(412) 341-1515

LDAA has for many years been a primary source of support
and information for children, adults, and professionals interested in the needs of those affected by learning disabilities. In
addition to its advocacy efforts both locally and nationally,
LDAA publishes newsletters and holds annual national conferences.

NCLD
National Center for Learning Disabilities
381 Park Avenue South, Suite 1420
New York, New York 10016
(212) 545-7510

NCLD was organized to provide public awareness about learning disabilities to enable both children and adults to achieve
their fullest potential. Membership benefits include subscrip-
tions to NCLD publications and announcements about regional
and national conferences.

NICHY
National Information Center for Children and Youth with
Disabilities
NICHY
P.O. Box 1492
Washington, D.C. 20013-1492

NICHY is a national clearinghouse for information on learning disabilities, attention deficit disorders and related conditions for children and adults.

Vendors

ADD WareHouse
300 Northwest 70th Avenue
Plantation, Florida 33317
(800) 233-9273 Voice (954) 792-8545 Fax
Internet: http://www.addwarehouse.com

ADD WareHouse publishes and distributes books, videos, and assessment products on attention deficit disorders.

Newsletters and Journals

ADDendum
c/o Chesapeake Psychological Services
5041 A Backlick Road
Annondale, VA 22003

ADDult Support Network
2620 Ivy Place
Toledo, OH 43613

ATTENTION!
CHADD
499 N.W. 70th Avenue, Suite 101
Plantation, Florida 33317
(305) 587-3700

CHALLENGE
P.O. Box 448
West Newbury, MA 01985

Appendix G

Suggested Reading on
Adults and College Students with ADD

Barkley, R.A. (1990). <u>Attention deficit hyperactivity disorder:
A handbook for diagnosis and treatment</u>. New York:
Guilford Press.

Bramer, J.S. (1996). <u>Succeeding in college with attention
deficit disorders: Issues and strategies for students, counselors and educators</u>. Plantation, FL: Specialty Press, Inc.

Goldstein, S. (1996). <u>Managing attention disorders and learning disability in late adolescence and adulthood.</u> New York:
Wiley Interscience Press.

Gordon, M. & McClure, D. (1995). <u>The down and dirty guide
to adult ADD</u>. New York: GSI Publications, Inc.

Hallowell, E.M. & Ratey, J.J. (1994). <u>Driven to distraction</u>.
New York: Pantheon Books.

Hallowell, E.M. & Ratey, J.J. (1994). <u>Answers to distraction</u>.
New York: Pantheon Books.

Hartmann, T. (1993). <u>Attention deficit disorder: A different
perception</u>. Novato, CA: Underwood-Miller.

Hartmann, T. (1995). <u>ADD success stories</u>. Grass Valley, CA:
Underwood Books.

Kelly, K. & Ramundo, P. (1993). <u>You mean I'm not lazy, stupid or crazy?!</u> Cincinnati, OH: Tyrell & Jerem Press.

Kravets, M. & Wax, I. (1993). <u>The K & W guide to colleges for the learning disabled</u>. New York: Harper Collins.

Latham, P.S. & Latham, P. H. (Eds.). (1994). <u>Succeeding in the workplace</u>. Washington, D.C.: JKL Communications.

Nadeau, K.G. (1994). <u>Survival guide for college students with ADD or LD</u>. New York: Magination Press.

Nadeau, K.G. (Ed.). (1995). <u>Attention deficit disorder in adults</u>. New York: Brunner/Mazel.

Quinn, P.O. (1994). <u>ADD and the college student</u>. New York: Magination Press.

Solden, S. (1995). <u>Women with attention deficit disorder.</u> Grass Valley, CA: Underwood Books.

Weiss, G., & Hechtman, L. (1993). <u>Hyperactive children grown up</u> (2nd ed.). New York: Guilford Press.

Weiss, L. (1992). <u>Attention deficit disorder in adults</u>. Dallas, TX: Taylor Publishing Company.

Weiss, L. (1994). <u>Attention deficit disorder in adults workbook.</u> Dallas, TX: Taylor Publishing Company.

Wender, P. H. (1987). <u>The hyperactive child, adolescent and adult.</u> New York: Oxford University Press.

Cited References

Americans with Disabilities Act, 42 ASC § 12101 et seq. (1990).

American Psychiatric Association. (1968). <u>Diagnostic and statistical manual of mental disorders</u> (2nd ed.). Washington, DC: Author.

American Psychiatric Association. (1980). <u>Diagnostic and statistical manual of mental disorders</u> (3rd ed.). Washington, DC: Author.

American Psychiatric Association. (1987). <u>Diagnostic and statistical manual of mental disorders</u> (3rd ed., rev.). Washington, DC: Author.

American Psychiatric Association. (1994). <u>Diagnostic and statistical manual of mental disorders</u> (4th ed.). Washington, DC: Author.

Barkley, R.A. (1990). <u>Attention deficit hyperactivity disorder: A handbook for diagnosis and treatment</u>. New York: Guilford Press.

Barkley, R.A., Anastopoulas, A.D., Guevremont, D.C., et al. (1991). Adolescents with ADHD: Patterns of behavioral adjustments, academic functions and treatment utilizations. <u>Journal of American Academy of Child and Adolescent Psychiatry,</u> <u>30</u>, 572-761.

Barkley, R.A. and Murphy, K. (1995, June). ADHD behavior checklist for adults. The ADHD Report, 3(3), 1.

Bogdan, R.C., & Biklen, S.K. (1982). Qualitative research for education. Boston: Allyn & Bacon.

Brown, T. B. (1995). Differential diagnosis of ADD versus ADHD in adults. In K.G. Nadeau (Ed.), A comprehensive guide to attention deficit disorder in adults (pp. 93-108). New York: Brunner/Mazel.

CHADD (1993a). Educational rights for children with ADD. Plantation, FL: Author.

CHADD (1993b). CHADD facts, 5, Attention deficit disorders: An educator's guide. Plantation, FL: Author.

Copeland, E.D., & Copps, S.C. (1995). Medications for attention disorders (ADHD/ADD) and related medical problems. Plantation, FL: Specialty Press, Inc.

Dixon, E.B. (1995). Impact of adult ADD on the family. In K.G. Nadeau (Ed.), A comprehensive guide to attention deficit disorder in adults (pp. 236-259). New York: Brunner/Mazel, Inc.

Education, Department of (1993). 34 CFR §§ 101.1-104.61

Education. (1990, February 9). The Wall Street Journal Report, p. R6.

Feingold, B.F. (1975). <u>Why your child is hyperactive</u>. New York: Random House.

Fowler, M., with Barkley, R.A., Reeve, R., & Zentall, S. (1992). <u>CHADD educators manual</u>. Plantation, FL: CHADD.

Gorden, R.L. (1980). <u>Interviewing: Strategy, techniques, and tactics</u>. Homewood, IL: Dorsey Press.

Hallowell, E.M. (1995). Psychotherapy of adult attention deficit disorder. In K.G. Nadeau (Ed.), <u>A comprehensive guide to attention deficit disorder in adults</u> (pp. 146-167). New York: Brunner/Mazel, Inc.

Hartmann, T. (1993). <u>Attention deficit disorder: A different perception</u>. Novato, CA: Underwood-Miller.

Holkeboer, R. (1996). <u>Right from the start: Managing your college career</u> (2nd ed.). Belmont, CA: Wadsworth Publishing Co.

Hunt, R.D., Mindera, R.B., & Cohen, D.J. (1985). Clonidine benefits children with attention deficit disorder and hyper-activity: Report of a double-blind placebo-crossover thera-peutic trial. <u>Journal of the American Academy of Child and Adolescent Psychiatry</u>, <u>24</u>, 617-629.

Ingersoll, B. & Goldstein, S. (1993). <u>Attention deficit disor-der and learning disabilities: Realities, myths and contro-versial treatments</u>. New York: Doubleday.

Kelly, K., & Ramundo, P. (1993). <u>You mean I'm not lazy, stupid or crazy?!</u> Cincinnati, OH: Tyrell & Jerem Press.

Klein, R.G., & Mannuzza, S. (1991). Long-term outcomes of hyperactive children: A review. <u>Journal of the American Academy of Child and Adolescent Psychiatry</u>, <u>30</u>, 383-387.

Latham, P.S. & Latham, P.H. (1994a). <u>Higher education services for students with attention deficit disorder and learning disabilities: A legal guide</u>. Washington, DC: National Center for Law and Learning Disabilities.

Lietz, I. (1987). <u>How to take notes—the Cornell method</u>. Unpublished manuscript, Lansing Community College, Lansing, MI.

Martin, C.A., Welsh, R.J., McKay, S.E., & Barcuther, C.M. (1984). Hyperactivity (attention-deficit disorder). <u>Journal of Family Practice</u>, <u>19</u>, 367-380.

Murphy, K.R. (1992, Fall/Winter). Coping strategies for ADHD adults. <u>CHADDer Box</u>, p. 10.

Murphy, K.R. (1995). Empowering the adult with ADD. In K.G. Nadeau (Ed.), <u>A comprehensive guide to attention deficit disorder in adults</u> (pp. 135-145). New York: Brunner/Mazel, Inc.

Nadeau, K. G. (1994). <u>Survival guide for college students with ADD or LD</u>. New York: Magination Press.

Nadeau, K.G. (1995). ADD in the workplace. In K.G. Nadeau (Ed.), <u>A comprehensive guide to attention deficit disorder</u> (pp. 308-334). New York: Brunner/Mazel, Inc.

Parker, H.C. (1992, November/December). ADAPT (Attention deficit accommodation plan for teaching). <u>CHADDer Box</u>, p. 16.

Parker, H.C. (1992). <u>The ADD hyperactivity handbook for schools: Effective strategies for identifying and teaching students with attention deficit disorders in elementary and secondary schools</u>. Plantation, FL: Specialty Press, Inc.

Quinn, P. O. (1994). <u>ADD and the college student</u>. New York: Magination Press.

Rapoport, J. (1995, November). <u>New findings in brain development in children with ADHD</u>. Workshop presented at the CHADD (Children and Adults with Attention Deficit Disorder) National Convention, Washington, D.C.

Rehabilitation Act of 1973, 29 USC § 701 et seq. (1973).

Richard, M.M. (1992, October). Considering student support services in college selection. <u>CHADDer Box</u>, p.1.

Richard, M.M. (1995). Students with attention deficit disorder in postsecondary education. In K.G. Nadeau (Ed.), <u>A comprehensive guide to attention deficit disorder in adults</u> (pp. 284-307). New York: Brunner/Mazel, Inc.

Selkowitz, K. (1993). ADD is different for each person. ADDult News, 3, pp. 1-2.

Shepherd, I.R., Duston, R.L., Russell, K.S., & Kerr, L.E. (1992). ADA audit, transition plan and policy statement for higher education, manual and workbook. Washington, DC: Association of Community College Trustees, American Association of Community Colleges.

Silver, L.B. (1992). Attention-deficit hyperactivity disorder: A clinical guide to diagnosis and treatment. Washington, D.C.: American Psychiatric Press, Inc.

Weinstein, C.S. (1994). Cognitive remediation strategies. Journal of Psychotherapy Practice and Research, 3, 44-57.

Weiss, G., & Hechtman, L. (1993). Hyperactive children grown up (2nd ed.). New York: Guilford Press.

Weiss, L. (1992). Attention deficit disorder in adults. Dallas, TX: Taylor Publishing Company.

Wender, P. H. (1987). The hyperactive child, adolescent, and adult. New York: Oxford University Press.

Whitman, B.Y. (1991). Roots of organicity: Genetics and genograms. In P. J. Accardo, T.A. Blondis, & B.Y. Whitman (Eds.), Attention deficit disorders and hyperactivity in children (pp. 37-56). New York: Marcel Dekker.

Wilens, T., Spencer, T. & Biederman, J. (1995). Pharmacotherapy of adult ADHD. In K.G. Nadeau (Ed.),

A comprehensive guide to attention deficit disorder in adults (pp. 135-145). New York: Brunner/Mazel, Inc.

Zametkin, A.J., Nordahl, T.E., Gross, M., King, A.C., Semple, W.E., Rumsey, J., Hamburger, S., & Cohen, R.M. (1990). Cerebral glucose metabolism in adults with hyperactivity of childhood onset. New England Journal of Medicine, 323, 1361-1366.

Zametkin, A.J. (Speaker). (1991). Neurobiology of attention deficit disorders (Cassette Recording No. 91-2002). Plantation, FL: CHADD.

General References

Argus, K. (1993, January). Emerging from an academic
   cocoon. CHADDer Box, p. 8.

Barkley, R.A., Fisher, M., Edelbrock, C.S., & Smallish, L.
   (1990). The adolescent outcome of hyperactive children
   diagnosed by research criteria: I. An 8 year prospective
   follow-up study. Journal of the American Academy of
   Child and Adolescent Psychiatry, 29, 546-557.

Barkley, R.A. (Speaker). (1991, September). New ways of
   looking at ADHD (Cassette Recording No. 91-2001).
   Plantation, FL: CHADD.

Barkley, R. A. (Speaker). (1992, October). Attention defi-
   cit-hyperactivity disorder in adults. Workshop presented
   at the CHADD (Children with Attention Deficit Disorder) National Convention, Chicago, IL.

Borland, B.L., & Heckman, H.K. (1976). Hyperactive boys
   and their brothers: A 25 year follow-up study. Archives
   of General Psychiatry, 33, 669-675.

Bramer, J.S. (1994/1995). Attention deficit disorder: The
   college experience of seven adults (Doctoral dissertation,
   Michigan State University, 1994.) Dissertation Abstracts
   International, 55, 1838A.

Dawson, P. (1992, June). Helping children with attention deficits survive in the classroom: What does the school psychologist have to offer? <u>CHADDer Box</u>, p. 1.

Feldman, S., Denhoff, E., & Denhoff, E. (1979). The attention disorders and related syndromes outcome in adolescence and young adult life. In E. Denhoff & L. Stern (Eds.), <u>Minimal brain dysfunction: A developmental approach</u> (pp. 369-384). New York: Musson Publishers.

Gersch, F. (1993, November). Treatment of ADD in college students. <u>CHADDer Box</u>, pp. 10-11.

Gittleman, R., Mannuzza, S., Shenker, R., & Bonagura, N. (1985). Hyperactive boys almost grown up. <u>Archives of General Psychiatry, 42,</u> 937-947.

Greene, R. (1992, November/December). ADHD students and their teachers: The search for the right "match." <u>CHADDer Box</u>, p. 1.

Hallowell, E.M. (1991, April). The emotional experiences of attention deficit disorder. <u>CHADDer Box</u>, p. 6.

Hallowell, E.M., & Ratey, J.J. (1993, January). 50 tips on the management of adult attention deficit disorder. <u>CHADDer Box</u>, p. 1.

Hallowell, E.M. & Ratey, J.J. (1994). <u>Driven to distraction</u>. New York: Pantheon Books.

Hallowell, E.M. & Ratey, J.J. (1994). <u>Answers to distraction</u>. New York: Pantheon Books.

Hechtman, L. (1992). Long-term outcome of attention-deficit hyperactivity disorder. In M. Lewis & G. Weiss (Eds.), Child and adolescent psychiatric clinics of North America (pp. 325-334). Philadelphia: W.B. Saunders.

Henker, B., & Whalen, C.K. (1989). Hyperactivity and attention deficits. American Psychologist, 44, 216-223.

Hosie, T.W., & Erk, R.R. (1992). Attention deficit disorder. Guideposts. Alexandria, VA: American Counseling Association.

Johnson, M.J. (1992). ADD: A lifetime challenge (life stories of adults with attention deficit disorder). Toledo, OH: ADDult Support Network.

Kaplan, C.P., & Schachter, E. (1991). Adults with undiagnosed learning disabilities: Practice considerations. Families in Society: The Journal of Contemporary Human Services, pp. 195-202.

Klee, S.H., Garfinkle, B.D., & Beauchesen, H. (1986). Attention deficits in adults. Psychiatric Annals, 16, 52-56.

Klein, R.G. (Speaker). (1991, September). Childhood ADHD: Outcomes in adult adjustment (Cassette Recording No. 91-1901). Plantation, FL: CHADD.

Kramer, R.J. (1986). What are hyperactive children like as young adults? Journal of Children in Contemporary Society, 19, 89-98.

Kroeger, S. & Schuck, J. (1993). <u>Responding to disability issues in student affairs</u>. San Francisco: Jossey Bass.

Langan, J. & Nadell, J. (1980). <u>Doing well in college</u>. New York: McGraw Hill.

Latham, P.S. & Latham, P.H. (1994b). Legal rights of students with ADD. In P. O. Quinn (Ed.), <u>ADD and the college student</u> (pp. 85-96). New York: Magination Press.

Liebert, M.A. (1991, May). Coming out of the closet... Confessions of an ADD? mother. <u>CHADDer Box</u>, p. 8.

MacAulay, D.J., Reid, W.A., & Johnson-Fedoruk, G.M. (1991). Attention deficits in hyperactive children: Connecting psychological theory with classroom practice. <u>Canadian Journal of Special Education</u>, <u>7</u>, 132-142.

Mash, E.J. (1989). Treatment of child and family disturbance: A behavioral-systems perspective. In E.J. Mash & R.A. Barkley (Eds.), <u>Treatment of childhood disorders</u> (pp. 3-36). New York: Guilford Press.

McGee, R., & Share, D.L. (1988). Attention deficit disorder hyperactivity and academic failure: Which comes first and what should be treated? <u>Journal of American Academy of Child and Adolescent Psychiatry</u>, <u>27</u>, 318-325.

Michigan Department of Education. (1993). <u>Attention deficit hyperactivity disorder: ADHD task force report</u>. Lansing, MI: Author.

Miller, K. (1993, January 11). Attention-deficit disorder affects adults, but some doctors question how widely. The Wall Street Journal, p. 1B.

Murphy, S.T. (1992). On being LD: Perspectives and strategies of young adults. New York: Teachers College Press.

Nadeau, K.G. (1992, November/December). College guidelines for ADHD students. Challenge, pp. 5-6.

Nichamin, S.J., & Windell, J. (1984). A new look at attention deficit disorder. Clarkston, MI: Minerva Press.

Njiokiktjien, C. (1988). Attention deficit disorders. Pediatric behavioral neurology: Vol.1. Clinical Principles (pp. 254-265). Amsterdam: Suyi.

Quinn, P.O., & Stern, J.M. (1991). Putting on the brakes. New York: Magination Press.

Ranseen, J.D., & Campbell, D. (1995). Adult attention deficit disorder: What's in a name? NAN Bulletin, 12, 7-8.

Ratey, J.R. (1991, Fall/Winter). Paying attention to attention in adults. CHADDer Box, p. 13.

Ratey, J.R., Hallowell, E.M., & Leveroni, C.L. [1993?]. Pharmacotherapy for ADHD in adults. (Available from Adult ADD Association, 125 E. Sunset Dr. #640, Bellingham, WA 98226-3529.)

Richard, M.M., Carstens, J.B., & Chandler, D. (1992). College students with attention deficit disorder: A guide for faculty. Iowa City: University of Iowa Student Disability Services.

Silver, L.B. (1992). Diagnosis of attention-deficit hyperactivity disorder in adult life. In M. Lewis & G. Weiss (Eds.), Child and adolescent psychiatric clinics of North America (pp. 325-334). Philadelphia: W.B. Saunders.

Sloan, M.S., Assadi, L., & Linn, L. (1991). Attention deficit disorder in teenagers and young adults. Kalamazoo, MI: Minerva Press.

Staff. (1991, October). ADD adult strategies: one success story. CHADDer Box, p. 8.

Staff. (1992, Fall/Winter). Testimony to the Senate and U.S. House of Representatives Subcommittee on Appropriations. CHADDer Box, p. 24.

Wallis, C. (1994, July 18). Life in overdrive. Time, pp. 42-50.

Ward, M.F., Wender, P.H., & Reimherr, F.W. (1993). The Wender Utah rating scale. American Journal of Psychiatry, 150, 885-890.

Weiss, G. (1990). Hyperactivity in childhood. New England Journal of Medicine, 323, 1413-1415.

Wender, P.H., Reimherr, F.W., & Wood, D.R. (1981). Attention deficit disorder (minimal brain dysfunction) in adults. Archives of General Psychiatry, 38, 449-456.

Werry, J.S., (1992). History, terminology, and manifestations at different ages. In M. Lewis & G. Weiss (Eds.), Child and adolescent psychiatric clinics of North America (pp. 297-310). Philadelphia: W.B. Saunders.

Werry, J.S., Elkind, G.S., & Reeves, J.C. (1987). Attention deficit, conduct, oppositional and anxiety disorders in childhood: III. Laboratory differences. Journal of Abnormal Child Psychology, 15, 409-428.

Wood, D. (1986). The diagnosis and treatment of attention deficit disorder, residual type. Psychiatric Annals, 16, 23-28.

Wolkenberg, F. (1987, October 11). Out of a darkness. New York Times Magazine, pp. 62-83.

Zametkin, A.J. (1989, November). The neurobiology of attention-deficit hyperactivity disorder: A synopsis. Psychiatric Annals, 19, 584-586.

Zentall, S.S., Falkenberg, S.D., & Smith, L.B. (1985). Effects of color stimulation and information on the copying performances of attention-problem adolescents. Journal of Abnormal Psychology, 13, 501-511.

Index

A

A Comprehensive Guide to Attention Deficit Disorder, 19
Accommodations,
   119, 120, 143, 147
ADD WareHouse, 168
ADDendum, 168
Adderall, 33
ADDult Support Network, 168
ADHD Behavior Checklist, 26–28
ADMIN, 145, 154
Admission,
   2, 68, 96, 123, 126, 151
Advocacy. *See* Self-advocacy.
Allergies, 38
American Psychiatric Association,
   43, 171
Americans with Disabilities Act
   (ADA), 116, 118, 138, 171
Amitriptyline (Elavil), 34
Anti-motion sickness, 39
Antidepressants, 34
   side effects of, 34–35
Antihypertensives, 35
Anxiety,
   14, 18, 23, 26, 30, 34, 45, 111, 148
Appointment book, use of, 125
Assessment procedures, 24–28
   in adults, 26
   of cognitive processing, 26
   of inattention and impulsivity, 26
Association on Higher Education
   and Disability, 145, 165
Attention Deficit Disorder (ADD),

and family life, 18
and social relations, 18
and the workplace, 19
causes of, 8–10
definition of, 6
diagnosis of, 22–24
impact on college students, 20
in adults, 15–18
outcomes in adults, 16–19
prevalence of in adults, 15
residual type, 12, 43
subtypes of, 12
undifferentiated attention deficit
   disorder, 12
with hyperactivity, 12
without hyperactivity, 12
Attention Deficit Disorder Association (ADDA), 165
Attention Deficit Disorder in Adults,
   45
Attention Deficit/Hyperactivity
   Disorder (AD/HD). *See also*
   Attention Deficit Disorder
   (ADD).
   combined type, 12–13
   hyperactive-impulsive type,
      12, 14
   in partial remission, 13
   inattentive type, 12–13
ATTENTION!, 168
Auxilliary aids, 117

B

Barkley, Russell, 7, 15, 17, 20–